CONTENTS

I THE ARTIST'S BEGINNINGS
13

II ARGENTEUIL, THE HIGH NOON OF IMPRESSIONISM
35

III "THIS STUNNING PARIS"
53

IV "ON THE BANKS OF THE SEINE AT VETHEUIL"
67

V "GIVERNY IS SPLENDID COUNTRY FOR ME"
83

VI HAYSTACKS, POPLARS, AND CATHEDRALS:
THE SERIES PAINTINGS
101

VII WATER LILIES: MONET'S FINAL MESSAGE
121

DOCUMENTS
129

Further Reading
168

Museums
168

List of Illustrations
169

Index
173

MONET
THE ULTIMATE IMPRESSIONIST

Sylvie Patin

DISCOVERIES

HARRY N. ABRAMS, INC., PUBLISHERS

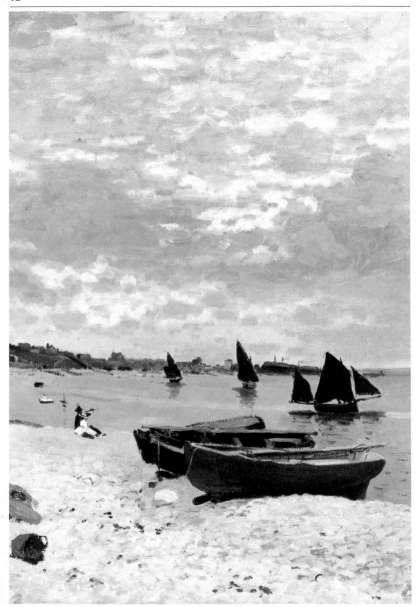

"A new name must be recorded here. We were not previously acquainted with Monsieur Claude Monet; a taste for harmonious coloring,…a bold way of seeing things and of capturing the observer's attention, these qualities Monsieur Monet already possesses to a high degree. We shall not forget him."

Critic Paul Mantz, "The Salon of 1865"
Gazette des Beaux-Arts, July 1865

CHAPTER I
THE ARTIST'S BEGINNINGS

Monet's canvases at the 1865 salon were entitled *The Pointe de la Hève at Low Tide* and *The Mouth of the Seine at Honfleur.* Two years later the artist was still painting yachts and the sea in *The Beach at Sainte-Adresse* (detail, left). Monet in around 1860 (right).

On 14 November 1840 a second son was born to Adolphe and Louise-Justine Monet of 45 Rue Laffitte, in the 9th arrondissement of Paris. Both parents were second-generation Parisians. They had the baby christened Oscar-Claude at the church of Notre-Dame-de-Lorette and called him Oscar for short. Oscar's early years were permeated with music, for his mother was a singer. No one has managed to ascertain what his father did, though he may have been in business.

Monet was born in Paris, but his childhood and youth were spent in Le Havre. His first "impressions" were of boats and the sea.

His precocious talent first emerged in caricatures of Le Havre citizens.

Around 1845 Adolphe Monet moved the whole family—his wife, his children, and his own parents—to Le Havre, in Normandy, on the northwest coast of France. His half-sister Marie-Jeanne Lecadre lived there, married to a wholesale grocer who took Adolphe into his business. Marie-Jeanne was to prove a kindly influence on her young nephew Oscar during his adolescence.

On 1 April 1851 Oscar Monet entered the Le Havre secondary school. "I was born unruly," he admitted later. "I could never bend to any rule, even as a very small child.... The school always seemed to me like a prison, and I could never resign myself to living there even for the space of four hours a day." In the school records he appears as "a very good-natured boy, who gets on well with his fellow pupils."

Oscar was already producing caricatures for his own amusement, but at the same time was receiving drawing lessons from Jean-François Ochard, a former pupil of Jacques-Louis David (1748–1825), Napoleon's court painter. The boy's first efforts (some dated 1857) are cartoon portraits of individuals, along with sketches of boats and landscapes that already reveal his taste for the outdoors, "when the sun was inviting, the sea beautiful, and it was so good to run along the cliffs."

1857: First Changes

On 28 January 1857 Oscar's mother died, and, now sixteen, he left school. His aunt Marie-Jeanne, left widowed and childless in 1858, took her nephew into her home. A friend of the painter Armand Gautier—and an amateur painter herself—she allowed him to continue his drawing lessons.

Oscar began to sell his caricatures, signed "O. Monet," at a stationer, framer, and ironmonger's shop, where they were displayed alongside the paintings of one Eugène Boudin, a former partner of the storekeeper. "It was at the framer's that I often exhibited my caricatures, and they earned me a certain notoriety in Le Havre and even a little cash," Monet was to say in 1922. "I also found Eugène Boudin there, who, at the age of about thirty, was beginning to make his presence felt.... At Boudin's suggestion I agreed to go out and work with him in the open air: I bought a box of paints and we went off to Rouelles [northeast of Le Havre]....

Boudin put up his easel and set to work.... For me it was like the rending of a veil; I understood, I grasped what painting could be;...my destiny as a painter opened up before me. If I have indeed become a painter, I owe it to Eugène Boudin.... With infinite kindness, he set about my education. Gradually my eyes were opened, and I understood

"I garlanded the margins of my textbooks and decorated the blue paper of my exercise books with fantastical ornamentation and drew the faces and profiles of my teachers, deforming them as much as I could."

Letter to François Thiébault-Sisson, 1900

nature; at the same time I learned to love her." The result of these lessons was *Landscape at Rouelles,* a work in the style of Boudin, which was shown at the Le Havre municipal exhibition in August and September 1858.

A drawing made in about 1856 of the semaphore and the François I tower at the entrance to the port of Le Havre.

Paris: Troyon and the Académie Suisse

Adolphe Monet applied to the city of Le Havre for a grant to enable his son to study painting in Paris but was turned down. So it was with the unaided support of his father—and the encouragement, no doubt, of his aunt—that Monet left for the capital in April 1859. He paid his first calls to the painters Armand Gautier and Constant Troyon; Troyon gave him valuable advice: "Start off by entering a studio where they do nothing but figurative work, studies from the nude: Learn to draw…but don't neglect painting.… Then do a few copies at the Louvre. Come and see me often: Show me your work."

At the 1859 Salon—the annual exhibition of "official" art—Monet saw the work of Troyon himself, as well as of the painters Charles-François Daubigny, Camille Corot, Eugène Delacroix, and Théodore Rousseau. In a letter he made an appeal to Boudin that presaged his own lifelong fascination with the sea. "There isn't one halfway decent seascape to be seen.… The fact is, there are simply no seascape painters, and you could go far in that line" (3 June). Monet was then working at the Académie Suisse, where he first met Camille Pissarro (who would later be known as the Father of the Impressionists).

The Algerian Experience

At the Salon, Monet noticed "a mass of magnificent paintings of the Orient; in all of them there is a certain grandeur and a warm light" (letter to Boudin, 3 June 1859). This admiration may partly

Left: A sketch by Monet, c. 1857, showing Boudin drawing outdoors.

This *Landscape at Rouelles* (left), dated 1858 by Monet, shows the artist's debt to Boudin: "I was interested in Boudin's frank approach to painting. I had become fascinated by his quick sketches, born of what I call immediacy" (letter to Gustave Geffroy, 8 May 1920). Boudin, whom Monet called the "King of the Skies," urged him to investigate nature.

explain the young man's voluntary enlistment in the first regiment of African light cavalry, which he joined in Algeria in June 1861. "How much my vision benefited by this," he was to say later. "The impression of light and colors I received there only fell into place afterward; but the germ of my future interests emerged in Algeria." On leave in Le Havre and Sainte-Adresse (just to the north) in the summer of 1862,

One of Boudin's "quick sketches" (below), *Boats at Low Tide.*

Monet became friendly with the Dutch painter Johan Barthold Jongkind. "From that time on Jongkind was my true master," he wrote. "I owe to him the final development of my painter's eye." Jongkind may also

have prompted Monet's aunt to help make it possible for Monet not to return to Algeria.

Monet in Paris

The painter Auguste Toulmouche, a medalist at the 1861 Salon and a friend of the Lecadres, kept an eye on the young man's work in Paris. On Toulmouche's recommendation, in late 1862 Monet entered the studio of Charles Gleyre, who was at the time also instructing Auguste Renoir and Alfred Sisley. A Swiss painter, Gleyre had earned a measure of fame with *Evening, or Lost Illusions*, shown at the 1843 Salon. Monet seems to have easily accepted the guidance of Gleyre, who was anything but authoritarian.

In March 1863 the young Frédéric Bazille—a fellow student working at Gleyre's—cited Monet as one of his "best friends among the daubers" in a letter to his father. The two went to Chailly-en-Bière outside Paris together. Bazille wrote to his mother: "I have spent eight days at the little village of Chailly near the forest of Fontainebleau. I was with my friend Monet, from Le Havre, who is rather good at landscapes. He gave me some tips that have helped me a lot." Monet stayed on alone at Chailly; on returning to Paris, he probably visited the official Salon and the Salon des Refusés (the exhibition of works rejected by the jury for the Salon), where the current sensation was Edouard Manet's *Déjeuner sur l'Herbe.*

After the summer holidays, Monet and Bazille returned to the capital and learned that Gleyre's studio was in danger of closing down. Monet left, and Bazille, Renoir, and Sisley soon followed suit.

Monet's First Youthful Masterpiece

In May 1864 Bazille and Monet were together in Normandy at Rouen, Sainte-Adresse, and Honfleur,

O f his first stay at Chailly, in 1863, Monet said, "I've found a thousand charms that I cannot resist here." On several occasions he painted the road between the village and Fontainebleau (*The Pavé de Chailly*, above); this version dates from around 1865.

C over of the Salon catalogue of 1865.

EXPLICATION
DES OUVRAGES
DE PEINTURE, SCULPTURE,
ARCHITECTURE,
GRAVURE ET LITHOGRAPHIE
DES ARTISTES VIVANTS,

RE 1er MAI
1865

Prix : 1 fr. 50 c.

PARIS

1865

where they stayed at the Auberge Saint-Siméon. Monet remained at Honfleur after Bazille's departure, writing to him enthusiastically on 15 July: "It's lovely here, my dear friend; every day I discover more and more beautiful things. It's enough to drive me mad, I want to paint everything so badly.... I have some wonderful projects."

At the end of that year Monet returned to Paris, where Bazille invited him to come and work in his studio at 6 Rue de Furstenberg. In 1865 the jury of the Salon accepted two landscapes by the "Le Havre painter," Monet's first official taste of success, and he was mentioned by the critic Paul Mantz in the *Gazette des Beaux-Arts* (July 1865).

Spring 1865 saw Monet back at Chailly. "The countryside is admirable," he wrote to Bazille. "Come as soon as you can." In the first days of May he told his friend of his plan to paint an immense composition (about 12 x 18 feet), entitled *The Picnic.* "I want you to

Manet's *Déjeuner sur l'Herbe* was shown at the Salon des Refusés in 1863. Though it is traditional in inspiration —based on the pastoral and bacchanalian scenes of classical masters, with touches of Titian, Giorgione, and Raphael —the most striking element of this "modern" composition is Manet's juxtaposition of a female nude with fully dressed men. Two years later Monet produced a painting of the same subject in a completely different style.

be here very much. I would like your opinion on the choice of landscape for my figures." That summer, he wrote again: "You promised to help me with my picture, you must come and pose for some of the figures. If you don't, the picture will be a failure; so I hope you will keep your promise."

Monet worked on the preparatory sketches at Chailly and started the painting in his Paris studio during the autumn. "I began just as everybody did then, by taking sketches from nature and composing the ensemble in my studio" (letter to the duke of Treviso, 1920). But the work remained unfinished; Monet probably gave up his idea of exhibiting this youthful masterpiece at the 1866 Salon after the painter Gustave Courbet came to see it and criticized it. Indeed, the large format (inspired by Courbet) was not representative of true plein air

" I think of nothing but my picture, and if I knew I was failing with it, I think I'd go mad," wrote Monet to Bazille of *The Picnic*, which he began in 1865. Only two large fragments of it survive (below). The smaller preparatory sketch (right) gives a general idea of the huge original composition. Below, left and right: A pencil sketch.

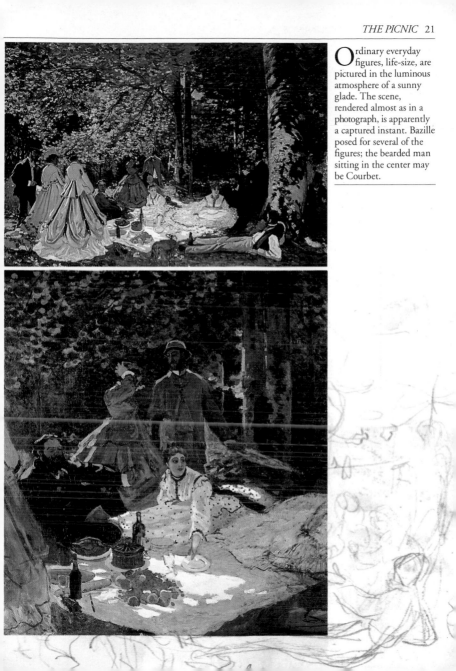

Ordinary everyday figures, life-size, are pictured in the luminous atmosphere of a sunny glade. The scene, rendered almost as in a photograph, is apparently a captured instant. Bazille posed for several of the figures; the bearded man sitting in the center may be Courbet.

landscape painting: The future lay with canvases
that could be painted outdoors, on the spot.

Woman in a Green Dress (or Camille)

Monet was soon back at work, preparing paintings
for the 1866 Salon. After he and Bazille left the Rue de
Furstenberg studio, he painted his life-size figure
Woman in a Green Dress. His model, Camille Doncieux,
was to become his mistress and later the first Madame
Monet. The painting was shown under the title *Camille*,
with a landscape of Chailly; it was noticed by the critics,
some of whom played with the names "Manet" and
"Monet." After *Woman in a Green Dress*, which was
painted indoors, Monet was eager to get out of the city
and make a new attempt at figures in a landscape.

Camille again served
as a model for
Women in the Garden
(1866–7, left). She is
the figure standing at
the far left.

"I Am Happier Than Ever"

The artist next installed himself at Sèvres, just outside Paris. "I am happier than ever," he wrote to Armand Gautier on 22 May. "I have made up my mind to retreat to the country; I am working a lot.... My success at the Salon secured me several picture sales." Soon he was having a trench dug in his garden so that he could work on the upper areas of a huge new canvas, *Women in the Garden*, by lowering it into the trench. This painting was taken to Honfleur, where he spent the summer and part of the winter. The painter Alexandre-Louis Dubourg mentions it in a letter to Eugène Boudin (2 February 1867) from that little Norman seaport:

A sumptuous silk dress and a jacket edged with fur make *Woman in a Green Dress* (1866, left and detail, above) a "typical Parisienne" of the time, in the words of Monet himself.

Although *Women in the Garden* was rejected by the 1867 Salon, Emile Zola remembered it a year later, when he wrote: "A painting of figures, women in light-colored summer dresses picking flowers along a garden walk; the sun falling straight on their skirts, which are brilliantly white; the warm shadow of a tree cutting across the path and their clothes like a broad gray blanket. Nothing could be stranger than this effect."

"Monet is still here, working away at enormous pictures.... He has one which is nearly three meters high and just as wide. The figures are slightly less than life-size, women in full summer dresses picking flowers in a garden. It's a canvas that he started in the open air."

In the first months of 1867 Monet joined Bazille at 20 Rue Visconti in Paris, where Renoir was also living.

That spring, Monet and Renoir worked on views of the city. Turned down by the jury of the 1867 Salon, *Women in the Garden* was bought by Bazille in January 1868 for 2500 francs, which he paid to his friend in installments of 50 francs per month.

"I Am with the Family, and As Well As I Can Be"

"People are kind to me, they admire my every brush stroke," wrote Monet to Bazille from Sainte-Adresse. "I have labored very hard, too: I have a score of paintings well under way, stunning seascapes, figures, gardens—everything, in fact." Among other things, he was working on *The Terrace at Sainte-Adresse.* At this time Monet's letters reveal "the deepest concern about Camille," whom he had left alone and pregnant in Paris because his family at Le Havre refused to receive her.

On 8 August 1867 Camille gave birth to a son, Jean. Four days later Monet wrote to Bazille, the child's godfather, to ask for help: "A fat and beautiful boy whom in spite of everything I feel I love, I don't know how. It pains me to think that his mother has nothing to eat."

After a brief visit to Paris that winter, Monet once again abandoned Camille and went to Le Havre, where he painted seascapes for the 1868 Salon. One of these was accepted, thanks to the efforts of Daubigny, who was a member of the Salon jury.

Monet's first seascapes often feature storms. The spray of the waves in *Rough Sea at Etretat* (1868–9, above) runs against the cliffs; silhouettes stand against the light-colored water. Left: The pencil drawing *Cliffs and the Sea* (c. 1865).

The daring construction of *The Green Wave* (1865, opposite) is reminiscent of a Japanese print.

Bathed in sunlight under fluttering flags, *The Terrace at Sainte-Adresse* (1867) shows the artist's family: His father (seated), perhaps his aunt Marie-Jeanne Lecadre, and (center) his distant cousin Jeanne-Marguerite Lecadre with an unidentified man. Here Monet captures the feel of the coast, where the intense sunshine flattens forms instead of rounding them out. The accessories help to illustrate life by the sea in summertime— the light-colored clothing of the women, the straw hats, the wicker chairs. The yachts, one of which stands out in the middle ground, go by on a blue-green sea, while farther out and on the horizon are steamships and all kinds of other vessels. This resplendent vision of a moment of happiness, in which flowers contrast with the water in a play of light and shadow, skillfully demonstrates the link among Monet's favorite motifs: "stunning seascapes and figures and gardens" (letter to Bazille from Sainte-Adresse, 25 June 1867).

"I am going into the country, which is so lovely now that I almost like it better in winter than in summer."
Letter to Bazille, Etretat, December 1868

In *The Magpie* (left, with details below left and opposite) Monet seems to take up a special challenge: how to use different shades of white to express the density and luminosity of a winter landscape, to which the dark bird stands in sharp contrast.

Between Le Havre, Etretat, and Paris

Probably on the recommendation of his friend Emile Zola, the novelist, Monet spent the spring of 1868 at the Auberge de Glotin, at Bennecourt near Bonnières-sur-Seine (west of Paris), with Camille and Jean. On 29 June

he wrote to Bazille: "I'm leaving for Le Havre this evening, to see if I can get my art lover to commission something…. My family refuses to do any more for me." Monet's "art lover" was Louis-Joachim Gaudibert, an industrialist who commissioned him to paint a portrait of his wife.

At Le Havre Monet showed five paintings at the International Maritime Exhibition, in which Antoine Vollon, Corot, Courbet, and Boudin also participated. The exhibition jury, one of whose members was Monet's old teacher Ochard, awarded him the silver medal. Also at this time Courbet introduced him to the novelist Alexandre Dumas.

In August Camille and Jean moved to Fécamp, still well away from the Monet family. Monet's pleas for money in his letters to Bazille begin to sound more urgent and emotional: "Consider my position. I have a sick child and no money whatsoever" (6 August 1868). In spite of his exhibition success, he continued to complain: "My painting isn't working at all, I no longer expect fame.... Everything looks black. On top of it all, there is still no money. Disappointments, affronts, hopes, more disappointments—there you have it, my friend" (letter to Bazille, October–November 1868).

But in December, at Etretat, the old ardor seems to have returned. "Here I am surrounded by everything I love. In the evening, my dear friend, I come back to my little house where there is a good fire and a good little family. If you could only see your godson, how sweet he is at present. My friend, it's quite lovely to watch the little creature grow, and God knows I am happy to have him. I plan to paint him for the Salon." This happy

The roof of a farmhouse where the painters met is depicted at the left in *Cart, Road Under Snow, Honfleur* (left, c. 1867). "I am still at Saint-Siméon, we are so happy here...we form a very agreeable little circle" (letter to Bazille, 26 August 1864).

interlude is commemorated by views of Etretat and by Monet's celebrated snowscape, *The Magpie*. Nevertheless, in 1869 his work was yet again turned down by the Salon.

June 1869 saw Monet living at the hamlet of Saint-Michel, on the Seine west of Paris. "Conditions are very good here," he wrote to Arsène Houssaye, who ran the magazine *L'Artiste* and had

bought his *Green Woman* (Monet's nickname for *Woman in a Green Dress*). "I have plenty of energy for work, but, alas, that fatal rejection has taken the bread from my mouth; despite my low prices, dealers and buyers turn their backs. It's sad how little people are interested in a work

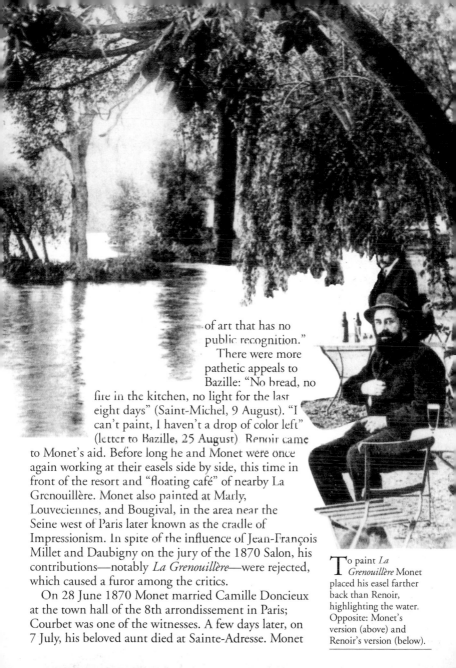

of art that has no public recognition."

There were more pathetic appeals to Bazille: "No bread, no fire in the kitchen, no light for the last eight days" (Saint-Michel, 9 August). "I can't paint, I haven't a drop of color left" (letter to Bazille, 25 August) Renoir came to Monet's aid. Before long he and Monet were once again working at their easels side by side, this time in front of the resort and "floating café" of nearby La Grenouillère. Monet also painted at Marly, Louveciennes, and Bougival, in the area near the Seine west of Paris later known as the cradle of Impressionism. In spite of the influence of Jean-François Millet and Daubigny on the jury of the 1870 Salon, his contributions—notably *La Grenouillère*—were rejected, which caused a furor among the critics.

On 28 June 1870 Monet married Camille Doncieux at the town hall of the 8th arrondissement in Paris; Courbet was one of the witnesses. A few days later, on 7 July, his beloved aunt died at Sainte-Adresse. Monet

To paint *La Grenouillère* Monet placed his easel farther back than Renoir, highlighting the water. Opposite: Monet's version (above) and Renoir's version (below).

The railroad allowed people to leave the French capital for a few hours and take the air in the countryside. The double-decker train cars outlined against the sky in *Train in the Countryside* (c. 1870, left and detail below) were used on the line from Paris west to Saint-Germain-en-Laye.

spent that summer at Trouville, in Normandy, where he worked on the beach and painted the *Hôtel des Roches Noires*. It was here that he heard of the declaration of war between France and Prussia. On 18 November Bazille was killed in battle. To avoid conscription Monet escaped by boat to England, where Camille and Jean later joined him.

"This Is a Man Who Will Be Greater Than Any of Us. Buy His Work"

It was with these words that Daubigny introduced Monet to the dealer who was to be the Impressionists' most loyal supporter: Paul Durand-Ruel. Their meeting was an event of great importance. A Monet canvas was shown at

" In the country, Claude Monet would seem to prefer an English park to a woodland glade. He takes pleasure in finding traces of mankind everywhere he goes, he wishes at all times to live among us. Like a true Parisian, he takes Paris to the country with him; he is unable to paint a landscape without including gentlemen and ladies in long dresses. Nature seems to lose its interest for him when it bears no imprint of our habits. "
Emile Zola
L'Evénement Illustré
24 May 1868

the first Durand-Ruel exhibition in London in December 1870. The following year, the dealer began buying Monet's canvases in quantity.

With Camille Pissarro, who was also in London, Monet visited the capital's museums, taking a particular interest in English landscape artists John Constable and J. M. W. Turner. Both Monet and Pissarro exhibited their work at the International Fine Arts Exhibition, which opened there on 1 May 1871.

Monet traveled to Holland. "What I have seen is much more beautiful than people say," he wrote to Pissarro from Zaandam (2 June 1871). Inspired by the houses, mills, and barges of the Netherlands, he wrote again on 17 June, "I am starting to work feverishly and have hardly any time to spare." As in London, he visited the museums, notably Amsterdam's Rijksmuseum. Finally, in the autumn, he arrived back in Paris.

During his first visit to London, Monet produced a few canvases of public gardens, such as *Green Park* (above). The lengthened format of the composition, which is handled like a sketch, with small dark figures, evokes the huge expanses of green that characterize London's parks. On the same visit he painted his beautiful *The Houses of Parliament and the Thames.*

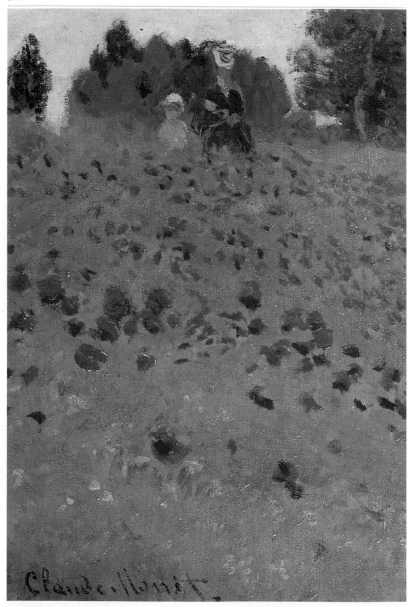

" We often see Monet and went to his housewarming recently. He is very well established and seems to have a strong desire to carve out a place for himself. I think he is destined to take one of the leading positions in our school. **"**

Eugène Boudin, 2 January 1872

CHAPTER II
ARGENTEUIL, THE HIGH NOON OF IMPRESSIONISM

In fields of burning red *Poppies* (1873, detail left) Camille Monet and her son Jean are seen walking. This landscape of the sunlit country around Argenteuil was one of the canvases that represented the artist's work at the First Impressionist Exhibition in 1874. Monet, about twenty-eight years old (right).

"Maison Aubry, Near the Almshouse at Porte Saint-Denis, Argenteuil"

This was the address Monet passed on to Pissarro on 21 December 1871, with the remark that "we are very busy moving in just now." The house (probably chosen for him by Manet) was just to the north of his previous one and close to the Seine, always a rich source of subject matter for Monet. He was greatly interested in the yachts, tugs, and the famous Argenteuil pool with its promenade, as well as the railway bridge and toll bridge, which were under reconstruction following the war of 1870.

I n the spring of 1872 Monet painted *Lilacs in Dull Weather* (above left, and detail below) and *Lilacs in Sunshine* (above), his first attempts at depicting a single subject in different lights.

Monet continued to paint flowers and work in his garden. Throughout the spring of 1872 he explored ways of representing human figures in landscapes, more often than not using Camille and Jean as models. While at Sainte-Adresse he had painted the Lecadre family from two different angles *(The Garden in Flower* and *Jeanne-Marguerite Lecadre in the Garden);* but in Argenteuil he twice took the same corner of the garden (a clump of lilacs) for his subject, depicting it in different lights. These two are the earliest forerunners of Monet's series paintings, which were to be so much a feature of his work in the 1890s. Apart from the Seine and his own garden, Monet amused himself painting the countryside around Argenteuil.

"His landscapes are illuminated by the sun.... Among others, there is a painting of a woman in white, seated in leafy shadows, whose dress is sprinkled with droplets of pure light."

Emile Zola
Le Messager de l'Europe
June 1876

"Monet seems happy with his lot, despite the difficulty he has in getting his paintings accepted," commented Boudin on 12 December 1872. All in all, however, it had been a productive year for the young artist, in terms of both work and money. He had sold thirty-eight canvases, including one to his brother Léon, one to Manet, five to the dealer Louis Latouche, and most importantly twenty-nine to Durand-Ruel, for a total of 12,100 francs. This information is provided by Monet's account book, which, together with Durand-Ruel's register, constitutes a vital source of information about the artist.

The next year saw Monet's profits from his work double. The average price for his paintings increased to 750 francs; again Durand-Ruel was a major purchaser. The first generation of Monet collectors included the banking brothers Albert and Henri Hecht and the critic

Monet continued his exploration of the human figure in *Girl Reading* (c. 1872–4), for which his model was probably Camille. The sketch-like quality of this picture lends it the force of a first impression; it delighted Zola when he saw it at the 1876 Second Impressionist Exhibition.

SOCIÉTÉ ANONYME
DES ARTISTES PEINTRES, SCULPTEURS, GRAVEURS, ETC.

Théodore Duret, author of *The Impressionist Painters*, a pamphlet that appeared in 1878. With the confidence born of this success, Monet soon began to drive much harder bargains.

In 1873 Monet returned to Normandy where he painted views of Etretat, Sainte-Adresse, and the port of Le Havre. Although it is dated "72," the canvas that has become immortal under the title *Impression, Sunrise* in fact belongs to this period.

1874: The First Impressionist Exhibition

Monet, having absorbed the lesson of his rejections by the Salons of 1869 and 1870, now gave up trying to sway the jury, as did Pissarro and Sisley. The idea of organizing an exhibition independent of the Salon had first been raised by Monet, Bazille, and their friends in 1867 but had been dropped for lack of funds. It now reemerged: "Everyone thinks it a good thing, only Manet is against it," wrote Monet to Pissarro on 22 April 1873. In a letter to the playwright and art critic Paul Alexis dated 7 May, Monet referred to the "society we are presently forming," and on 30 November he informed Pissarro "I have not forgotten our society, I am doing what I can." Like Pissarro, Edgar Degas, and Renoir, he was wholly dedicated to the cause.

After several reframings of the founding statute (during which Monet appears to have played the role of peacemaker), a "limited cooperative society of artist-painters, sculptors, engravers etc.," consisting of thirty members, was formed on 17 January 1874. The society's first exhibition was held from

"I sent something I did at Le Havre: The sun in the mist, and a few ships' masts.... They asked me its title for the catalogue, and I said: 'Call it *Impression*.'"
    Monet, quoted by the journalist Maurice Guillemot in *La Revue Illustrée*, 15 March 1898

L'Exposition

"What does this canvas mean? Look at the booklet. *Impression, Sunrise* [opposite, with detail]. *Impression*, just as I thought. I also said to myself, since I'm impressed, there must be some impression in it." It was in this mocking passage by the critic Louis Leroy in *Le Charivari*, 25 April 1874, that the term *Impressionism* originated.

. Monsieur le peintre impressionniste
- à la Morgue !

15 April to 15 May in premises belonging to the photographer Nadar (Félix Tournachon) at 35 Boulevard des Capucines in Paris.

The catalogue included sixty-five items by such artists as Boudin, Félix Bracquemond, Paul Cézanne, Edgar Degas, Armand Guillaumin, Edouard Lépine, Berthe Morisot, Pissarro, Renoir, and Sisley, to mention only a few. Some of the exhibitors (Boudin and Lépine, for example) were also present at the official Salon, which opened two weeks later. Numbers 95 to 103

in the catalogue were works by Monet (sometimes with two pictures listed under the same number). They included *Poppies*, a seascape of Le Havre, *Boulevard des Capucines*, the interior scene with Camille and Jean (*Luncheon*, 1868) that had been refused by the 1870 Salon—was this perhaps a defiant challenge to the jury?—and, above all, *Impression, Sunrise*, which, like most of the work in this exhibition, was more focused on capturing the experience of a moment than realistically rendering a scene.

The critics immediately lashed out at the rebel group, focusing their comments on Monet. In the 25 April issue of *Le Charivari*, Louis Leroy disparagingly entitled his article "Exhibition of the Impressionists" (thereby coining the term), while Emile Cardon wrote about the "School of the Impression" (*La Presse*, 29 April). The more indulgent Armand Silvestre, commenting in *L'Opinion Nationale* on 22 April, allowed himself to be interested in the "vision of things" displayed by Monet, Pissarro, and Sisley; nevertheless,

he wrote, "It is an effect of impression alone that this vision

In the garden of Monet's first house at Argenteuil his son Jean sits engrossed with his toys, while in the background are two female figures whose pale-colored dresses stand out against the foliage. This light-filled canvas, entitled *Luncheon* (c. 1873), seems to exude well-being. Anecdotal details combine to express the art of living in the country. The abundance of flowers, the attractiveness of the clothes, the whiteness of the tablecloth, the arrangement of the food (especially the fruit bowl), and the refined cups and coffeepot. At the same time there is something strange about the painting, for Monet has chosen to paint the scene only after the meal has ended. The diners have left the table, the parasol lies on the bench, and the hat hangs forgotten from a bough of the tree; all this creates an enigmatic atmosphere, as of a happiness that is fleeting. This composition, the format of which is unusual for Monet's Argenteuil period, figured in the 1876 Second Impressionist Exhibition under the title *Decorative Panel*.

E douard Manet
recorded his friend's
domestic life in *The
Monet Family in the
Garden* (1874, top), a
carefully worked
composition that includes
Monet himself, gardening
in the background.
Renoir's spontaneous
version of the same
subject shows only Mme.
Monet and Jean (left).

seeks to discover; expression is left to adepts of the line."

The society was dissolved in December—but
Impressionist exhibitions resumed two years later
in 1876.

The Halcyon Days of Impressionism

After the tension surrounding the exhibition, Monet
retired to Argenteuil for a well-deserved rest. His friends
were frequent visitors; Manet, who contributed to the

household expenses, painted *The Monet Family in the Garden*, while Renoir executed his canvas *Mme. Monet and Her Son* in the same surroundings. The Seine, with its bridges and regattas, was still a favorite subject for painters, but the town of Argenteuil itself was by no means forgotten *(The Grand-Rue)*. During a long painting campaign carried out on his own, Monet concentrated particularly on winter landscapes.

In the autumn of 1874 the painter

moved yet again, this time to "2 Boulevard Saint-Denis, opposite the station, a pink house with green shutters." This living situation was a foretaste of his future house at Giverny. The garden appeared in his 1875 work and was to be even more prominent the following year.

The fine weather in the spring of 1875 also saw Monet on the riverbank at nearby Petit-Gennevilliers and out in the flowering meadows with Camille and Jean.

"Although I Have Faith in the Future, the Present Is Very Hard to Bear" (Letter to Manet, 28 June 1875)

With Durand-Ruel obliged first to cut back, then temporarily suspend his purchases, Monet had to count on the new buyers of Impressionist work, whose names now began to appear in his account books. The main purchasers were opera baritone Jean-Baptiste Faure and textile merchant Ernest Hoschedé, a passionate collector who bought *Impression, Sunrise* in May 1874 for the exceptional price of 800 francs. Still, Monet's earnings for 1874 (a total of 10,554 francs)

If Manet's qualities as a colorist are obvious in *The Monet Family*, the painting's linear precision shows that he could also be a great draftsman. The same talent appears in his China ink–wash study of Monet, *Head of a Man* (above). The hat tilted backward, the incisive, skillful brushwork, and the intensity of the black beard emphasize Monet's forceful profile.

In 1872 Renoir painted intimate portraits of Camille (opposite, right) and Claude Monet (left). Here Monet is caught in a humdrum pose, smoking his pipe and reading a newspaper.

From the River at Argenteuil to the Flower Garden

In 1874 Manet painted *Monet Painting in His Studio-Boat* (opposite, above). This vessel, which Monet himself depicted several times (opposite, below, *The Studio-Boat*, c. 1874), had been adapted by the artist for his work on the Seine. *Regattas at Argenteuil* (1872, above, with details below) demonstrates Monet's technical mastery. Here touch and color are fragmented to convey the play of the quivering water surface and the reflected sails.

Overleaf: In *Monet Painting in His Garden at Argenteuil*, Renoir portrayed his friend at his easel (above right). Monet's version of the same garden, *The Artist's House at Argenteuil* (left, with details), places the silhouette of Jean in the center, framed by small urns that heighten the decorative effect of the scene. The child, who is dressed with studied elegance, is a strong presence, though seen only from behind. The leaves and flowers, with their blend of greens and reds, are reminiscent of *The Terrace at Sainte-Adresse*, as are the pools of light and shadow on the path.

Claude Monet

were well below that of the previous year.

On several occasions in 1875 he applied to Manet for help: "My color-box will stay closed for a long time now, if I can't get out of this mess," he wrote. Each time his faithful friend answered the call with cash advances, just as Bazille had done before him.

On 24 March 1875 a sale was arranged (probably by Renoir) at the Drouot auction rooms, with Durand-Ruel as auctioneer; 163 works by Renoir, Morisot, Sisley, and Monet went under the hammer for very low prices, amid a torrent of sarcasm. Monet's twenty canvases failed to reach even 200 francs. While his income was very small, the circle of buyers (Faure, Emile Blémont, Ernest May, Henri Rouart, Victor Chocquet) who dealt with him on a private basis continued to grow, heralding the wider recognition of his talent.

The Second Impressionist Exhibition took place in April 1876 at the Durand-Ruel Gallery, 11 Rue Le Peletier in Paris. The catalogue featured eighteen pictures by "Monnet" (*sic*). While many critics arrived ready to mock, the press generally greeted this show more favorably than that of 1874.

The writers Armand Silvestre, Jules-Antoine Castagnary, and Stéphane Mallarmé were full of praise, and Emile Zola saluted Monet's major role: "Without a doubt, Claude Monet is the leader of the group. His brush is distinctive for its extraordinary brilliance."

Fresh buyers began to emerge, among them painter and collector Gustave Caillebotte and doctor Georges de Bellio. Both became financial and moral mainstays for Monet.

The amenities of Argenteuil became accessible through the growing new railroad system. *The Railway Bridge, Argenteuil* (c. 1873, below, with details) employed a subject Monet found just as suitable as gardens and yachts.

The passage of a train over the bridge, crossing the countryside obliquely, is caught as if in a photograph.

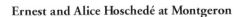

Ernest and Alice Hoschedé at Montgeron

When Monet was scouting for subject matter away from Argenteuil (notably in Paris, during the spring of 1876) Ernest Hoschedé invited him to decorate the Château de Rottembourg, at Montgeron (southeast of Paris), which

In this version (1874) the massive architecture is broken up by the combined action of light and water.

A lice Hoschedé, photographed on 1 January 1878 with Jean-Pierre Hoschedé, who was probably Monet's child.

his wife Alice had inherited.

For the main salon of the château, Monet executed four paintings illustrating the two seasons during which he stayed there: the summer, with *Turkeys, Corner of a Garden at Montgeron* (or *The Dahlias*), and *The Pool at Montgeron;* and the autumn, with *The Hunt* (or *Avenue in the Park, Montgeron*). It is probable that he visited Gustave Caillebotte, who owned property near the River Yerres, at this time.

The following year, on 20 August 1877, Alice Hoschedé gave birth to her sixth child, Jean-Pierre, who is thought to have been Monet's son. In later life Jean-Pierre liked to refer to his physical resemblance to Monet, about whom he wrote a book.

"We Must Leave Argenteuil"

After his interlude at Montgeron, Monet returned to Argenteuil and a host of money worries. "Unless there is a sudden torrent of rich patrons, we are going to be put out of this nice little house…where I have worked so well…and yet I was full of enthusiasm and had plenty of projects" (letter to Dr. de Bellio, c. 25 July 1876). The first months of 1877 were taken up by a painting of the Gare Saint-Lazare and the preparation of the Third Impressionist Exhibition, in which, among other things, Monet showed *Turkeys.*

Life at Argenteuil had involved major expenses; despite the large income recorded in his accounts, the painter was heavily in debt and worried that his furniture would be removed and sold if he failed to satisfy his creditors. To Dr. de Bellio he wrote that "fresh misfortunes have befallen me; as if it were not enough to be short of money, my wife has now fallen ill."

On 15 January 1878 he told his friend: "In two days, that is *the day after tomorrow,* we must leave Argenteuil; and to do that, I must pay my debts." It is very likely that Caillebotte finally gave Monet a cash advance, which made it possible for him to go. Even so, he had to leave *The Picnic* with his landlord as a guarantee.

The fate of this picture—it was rolled up and stored in a cellar—symbolized the end of an era. (Later, Monet insisted on recovering *The Picnic,* which he saw as a link with his youth and the most spectacular illustration of his early years as an artist.)

In 1876 Monet returned to large-format work with his decorative panels for the Château de Rottembourg, seen here in the background of *Turkeys.* This is a surprising subject, with a daring perspective borrowed from Japanese prints. The turkey in the foreground adds to the immediacy of the scene.

"Paris! You must go to Paris! Young men, writers, and artists who breathe the stifling air of the provinces are obsessed with this idea. Claude Monet…wanted to be in Paris so he could see the museums and exhibitions, meet other painters, and show his work at the Salon. Later, nearly all of them (and Monet in particular) were glad to regain their solitude…and draw one or two secrets from the sphinx that is nature."

Critic Gustave Geffroy, *Claude Monet,* 1922

CHAPTER III
"THIS STUNNING PARIS"

Crowds, as in *Rue Montorgueil, Fête of 30 June 1878* (detail, opposite), were Monet's principal subject matter in Paris. "This city frightens me," he wrote to Geffroy. Monet in around 1875 (right).

"All the Beautiful Things I See in Paris"

For Monet, a Parisian by birth who had spent his childhood and adolescence at Le Havre, the French capital seemed rich in contrasts in comparison to the countryside and the sea. He would always be drawn to it. In one of his earliest known letters, written to Boudin from Paris on 3 June 1859, Monet describes the first impact on the young artist of "this stunning Paris."

Even at a young age, he seemed to have been especially aware of the beauty of the Seine and its banks. "I rose early, I had a delightful walk along the quays and through the Tuileries, it was charming, and I was entirely happy" (letter to Armand Gautier, 7 March 1864). On 20 May 1867 he wrote to Bazille: "Renoir and I are still working on our views of Paris," referring to the pictures the two were doing from the Louvre.

Boudin, who lived in Paris but never painted it, was fully aware of his friend's talent. "We were talking of Monet," he wrote on 18 January 1869. "At a dealer's on the Rue Lafayette there is a view of Paris by him that would be worthy of the great masters, if the details were on a par with the ensemble. That boy has what it takes.…"

Run Away from Paris…or Stay There?

In December 1868, Monet wrote to Bazille from Normandy describing his hesitations about Paris. "I don't envy you being there… don't you think that one does better when one is alone with nature? I'm sure of it. One's too preoccupied with what one hears in Paris…and what I do here will at least have the merit of being unlike anyone else's work…because it'll simply be the expression of what I personally

"I have the honor of requesting a special authorization to paint views of Paris from the windows of the Louvre, and notably from the outside colonnade, since I wish to try a view of Saint-Germain l'Auxerrois.**"**
Letter to Count Emilien de Nieuwerkerke, Superintendent of Fine Arts, 27 April 1867

The young Monet obstinately insisted on observing Saint-Germain l'Auxerrois (1867, left) from a high elevation, painting the animation of Paris in the midst of a play of light and shade.

felt myself. I really believe I won't come to Paris for long periods now, no more than a month each year."

But there was one particular factor that led Monet to take a radical change of course. On 2 June 1869, shortly after moving to the hamlet of Saint-Michel near Bougival, we find him writing to Arsène Houssaye: "You advised me to come and live in Paris, where it would obviously be easier for me to profit from what talent I possess. The rebuff by the Salon has completely made up my mind…we are now settled in, I am in excellent surroundings and keen to work." On 25 April Boudin had written: "Monet's two paintings have been *rejected* this year, but he has avenged himself by showing a study of Sainte-Adresse at one of our dealers, Latouche. The artistic fraternity is flocking to see it. There's been a crowd in front of Latouche's window…. Its unexpectedness and violence have gained Monet a *fanatical* following among the young."

Monet often left Bougival to see his friends in Paris, and may even have posed with them for Bazille's *Studio on the Rue de la Condamine* (1870). He certainly appears in *The Batignolles Studio* (1870) by Henri Fantin-Latour. Paris was also the setting for his marriage to Camille Doncieux on 28 June 1870.

In 1872, working with Renoir (c. 1875, above) once again, he painted the Pont-Neuf (photograph opposite) and other Paris scenes.

The Studio on the Rue de l'Isly

On his return from England in the autumn of 1871 Monet stayed for a while at the Hôtel de Londres et de New York near the Gare Saint-Lazare, then an area much favored by artists and writers. He frequently worked in Armand Gautier's former studio, which he kept until 1874, giving as his address 8 Rue de l'Isly. The railroad station itself became a subject for him in 1877. For the time being, he and Renoir worked on their versions of the *Pont-Neuf* (1872).

Monet began by portraying the image of traditional Paris: the banks of the Seine, the quays, and the bridges in the heart of the capital. Next, in 1873, he painted two pictures of the *Boulevard des Capucines* as seen from

Above: From a window at 35 Boulevard des Capucines (the studio of the photographer Nadar and site of the 1874 First Impressionist Exhibition) Monet painted the busy Paris of the boulevards. He conveyed the crowd of pedestrians with diminutive dark touches, which excited the irony of Louis Leroy: "Here is an impression which baffles me... please tell me the meaning of these innumerable black dribbles at the bottom of the canvas" (*Le Charivari*, 25 April 1874). A note of color is supplied by the pink balloons.

Bazille (opposite): A self-portrait in pencil.

One of the two *Boulevard des Capucines* (1873, left) was shown at the 1874 exhibition. Though mocked by Leroy, it was admired by the critic Ernest Chesneau: "Never has the prodigious animation of the street, the antlike scurrying of the crowd on the pavement, the carriages on the roadway, the shimmering of the trees on the boulevard amid its dust and light, never before has the elusiveness of movement been caught and held in its fluidity as in this extraordinary *Boulevard des Capucines*" (*Paris-Journal*, 7 May 1874).

Nadar's studio, in which he expressed his fascination with Baron Haussmann's new rebuilding of Paris; it is "this stunning Paris" with its happy, colorful crowds that now appears in his canvases. One of these scenes was shown in the First Impressionist Exhibition of 1874, where it provoked the scorn of Louis Leroy and other critics.

Monet's representation of these scenes of contemporary life answers to the criterion of "modernity—that transitory, fugitive element," as advocated by the poet Charles Baudelaire in 1863. These "urban landscapes" seen from above, these effects of mounting perspective, were also sought by Caillebotte and Pissarro. They point up the double influence on the Impressionists of the first photographs, with their instantaneous quality, and Japanese prints, with their unusual viewpoints and flat planes of color.

Japonisme and French Painting

Monet seems to have discovered Japanese prints in London, and then in Zaandam, well before they became familiar to him in Paris. On 31 March 1875 the writer Edmond de Goncourt described in his *Journal* "this great Japanese movement, which today is overflowing from painting into fashion. It began with a few originals, like my brother and I...and was taken up after us by the group of Impressionist painters." The "japonisme" that enthralled Paris is brilliantly revealed in Monet's canvas entitled *La Japonaise* (which is sometimes called *Japonnerie*, as in the catalogue of the Second Impressionist Exhibition, 1876, or *Japonerie*, as at the Drouot auction of 14 April of the same year).

Monet's Public Gardens

If the gardens of Monet's various houses around Argenteuil can be seen as a kind of injection of town into country, his renderings of parks in Paris produce exactly the opposite effect. Ever since Sainte-Adresse he had been passionately interested in gardens, and now he dedicated several paintings to the two great promenades of elegant and fashionable Paris society: the Tuileries and the Parc Monceau.

In the spring of 1876 Monet executed four views of the Tuileries (Manet and Renoir had done the same before him) as seen from Chocquet's apartment at 198 Rue de Rivoli. Three of these views were sold, to Dr. de Bellio, Ernest May, and Caillebotte.

At the Third Impressionist Exhibition of 1877, three pictures of the Tuileries were exhibited alongside a view of the Parc Monceau; in 1878 Monet completed a second version of this park, near which Ernest Hoschedé resided.

"I Have Just Taken Steps to Obtain Leave to Paint in the Gare Saint-Lazare"

At about the time Monet told the publisher Georges Charpentier that he had rented a new studio in Caillebotte's name at 17 Rue Moncey near the Gare Saint-Lazare (17 January 1877), Monet embarked on a series of views of both the interior and exterior of the

In 1919 Monet referred to the canvas above, which was painted in 1875–6: "*La Japonaise...* a Parisienne in Japanese costume. My first wife was the model." More than just an imitation of the Japanese print style, the painting is a brilliant example of the japonisme of the era, in its emphasis on decorative accessories (the actor's costume or kimono, fans, and blond wig).

Parc Monceau (1878), another study of light filtering through trees.

railway station. He showed the trains that traveled to the places he had depicted outside Paris; he was less interested in the human presence than in the spectacle of modern technology in action.

This choice of subject may seem odd for a painter of the outdoors. Nevertheless, by taking an interest in a place so thoroughly characteristic of the epoch, Monet showed himself to be a true man of his time. The Gare Saint-Lazare—omnipresent in Zola's novel *La Bête Humaine* (1889–90), in which the writer gives a major role to a steam engine called Lison, and analyzed by Marcel Proust in his *Remembrance of Things Past*—represented the new industrialization and the kind of glass and metal architecture exemplified by London's Crystal Palace. It was the "gateway to the city," the departure point for the various railway lines leading out

The Gare Saint-Lazare. Left to right: A view from outside the station, the arrival of a train, and the tracks running under the nearby Pont de l'Europe.

A preparatory sketch for a painting of the Gare Saint-Lazare (c. 1877, opposite).

With *The Gare Saint-Lazare* (1877) Monet tackled the combined themes of the building, with its metal-and-glass roof, and the steam engine. The glass canopy creates a symmetrical composition centered on the dark, moving train. In the background the sunlight appears to fragment the facades of the buildings. In train stations, "palaces of modern industry, where the religion of the century, that of the railways, is made manifest," in these "cathedrals of the new humanity" (Théophile Gautier), Monet was enchanted by the light playing on clouds of steam escaping from the engines.

"Monsieur Claude Monet is the most marked personality in the group. This year he has exhibited some superb railway station scenes. In these one can hear the rumbling of the trains and see the smoke rolling and flooding through the huge sheds. Here is the painting of today, in these beautiful, broad, modern canvases. Our artists must look to the poetry of railway stations, as their fathers sought that of forests and rivers."

Emile Zola
Le Sémaphore de Marseille
19 April 1877

to such meccas of Impressionism as Bougival, Louveciennes, Argenteuil, Vétheuil, Pontoise, Giverny, and Normandy. The station was not the only such subject to attract the Impressionists' attention; the curious iron girders of the nearby Pont de l'Europe ("which is amazing on account of its bizarre shape and its sheer size," according to an 1867 guide) were an inspiration to Manet and Caillebotte as well as to Monet.

In addition to his canvases of Paris public gardens, Monet presented eight views of the Gare Saint-Lazare (the eighth was not included in the catalogue) at the Third Impressionist Exhibition of April 1877.

"I Am a Countryman Again"

Obliged to leave Argenteuil in January 1878, Monet returned to Paris again, staying with Camille and Jean for several months at 26 Rue d'Edimbourg and keeping the studio on the Rue Moncey. On 30 March he wrote to the collector Ernest May, "My wife has just had another baby [17 March], and I find myself penniless and unable to pay for the medical care that both mother and child must have." Appeals were also made to another patron, Eugène Murer, and to his friend Zola; finally the family's old friend Manet, who had acted as a witness at the registration of birth of the new baby, Michel, once again came forward with the necessary help.

Monet now returned to the theme of gardens; ten paintings showing the banks of the Seine at the Ile de la Grande Jatte gave an intimation of the work that was still to come.

Five years after painting *Boulevard des Capucines,* he once again captured on canvas the bustle of Paris on a national holiday, this time in the year of the Universal Exposition (1878). The crowds in the flag-bedecked *Rue Montorgueil* and *Rue Saint-Denis* are Monet's brilliant farewell to Paris, which now disappears from his work forever. "I am a countryman again, and I shall not come to Paris save at intervals, to sell my pictures," he wrote to Duret on 8 February 1879.

Above: An 1877 caricature in which a pregnant woman is turned away from the Impressionist exhibition for fear of a miscarriage.

"I loved flags. The first national holiday of 30 June, I went walking in Rue Montorgueil: The street was decked with pennants, there were lots of people; I saw a balcony and went up to it" (letter to René Gimpel, October 1920). *Rue Montorgueil* (left) is another view painted from above, with a rising perspective borrowed from Japanese prints and photography.

Opposite: Manet photographed by Nadar, c. 1864.

"You may have heard that I have pitched my tent on the banks of the Seine at Vétheuil, in a ravishing place" (letter to Eugène Murer, 1 September 1878). The river became the subject of a series of winter landscapes (Ice Floes). These canvases are filled with Monet's sadness at the death of Camille, an event that marked the end of his youth and came at a time when the Impressionist movement was disintegrating.

CHAPTER IV
"ON THE BANKS OF THE SEINE AT VETHEUIL"

The Seine at Vétheuil (1879): Here Monet has opted for a vertical format, unusual for the Vétheuil period. The horizon divides the composition between sky and water in a harmony of blues and greens. Monet in around 1879 (right).

The village of Vétheuil, on the banks of the Seine, northwest of Paris, is beautifully situated. From a slight elevation, it dominates a loop of the river that is sprinkled with wooded islands. This distinctive landscape was bound to attract Monet. First of all he set about painting the houses grouped around the church.

His tireless attempts to master the constant variations of light playing over the same scene indicate Monet's fondness for his adopted village. Scarcely changing the position of his easel at all, he persisted at Vétheuil in his study of light and new compositional formats. The resulting canvases were quickly sold to Caillebotte, Duret, and de Bellio.

"I Cannot Hope to Earn Enough Money from My Paintings to Pay for Our Life Here at Vétheuil"

At Vétheuil Monet and his family shared a house with Alice and Ernest Hoschedé and the two couples' six

Several times during his first winter at Vétheuil, Monet painted the village under snow: *The Church at Vétheuil, Snow* (1878–9, top).

To obtain a panoramic view of Vétheuil, Monet used his studio-boat on the Seine, set up his easel on one of the islands, or crossed the river and worked from the far bank (left). In these landscapes, which at first seem similar, a different effect appears at each attempt—the effect of snow (opposite) and *The Seine at Vétheuil, Effect of Sunshine After Rain* (left). Here the artist applies a technique he had perfected at Argenteuil: The fragmented brushwork simulates moving water, and the architectural outlines resist the dissolving effect of light.

children, partly in an attempt to save money. The house had an orchard leading down to the river, where Monet moored his studio-boat. Later, in December 1878, the families moved to more comfortable quarters, and in Paris, meanwhile, Monet forsook his studio on the Rue Moncey for another at 20 Rue de Vintimille.

The house at Vétheuil enabled him to concentrate as never before on his vision of nature, without the

distractions of city life, but it also contributed to Monet's growing isolation from his Impressionist friends. He did agree to submit twenty-nine works to the Fourth Impressionist Exhibition at 28 Avenue de l'Opéra in Paris; but "it was much against my will—and only to avoid the charge of treachery" (letter to Murer, 25 March 1879), and also because he

At Vétheuil (photograph above) Monet's main preoccupations were the interplay of earth and sky and the landscape mirrored by the river.

desperately needed the money.

Unable to pay either his rent or his debt to Manet for the expenses of the move, Monet considered uprooting his family yet again (letter to Ernest Hoschedé, 14 May 1879): "Only I know how deep are my anxieties and the trouble I have in finishing my canvases, which don't satisfy me, and indeed please very few other people. I am totally discouraged.... I must accept the hard fact that I cannot hope to earn enough money from my paintings to pay for our life here at Vétheuil.... We can't be very good company for you and Madame Hoschedé, myself more and more embittered, and my wife nearly always sick.... Our departure would be a relief for everyone in the house, even though I believed I could create dreams of work and happiness here.... "

"My Poor Wife Died This Morning"

In the letters he wrote to de Bellio, Monet revealed his concern about the health of Camille, who had been "extremely frail" ever since the birth of Michel. Finally, on 5 September 1879 he wrote, "My poor wife died this

Monet rarely painted flowers indoors, but autumn prompted him to paint *Chrysanthemums* (1878, above left).

morning.... I am filled with dismay to find myself alone with my poor children. I want to request another service of you: to redeem the medallion we pawned at the Mont de Piété with the enclosed money. It is the only souvenir that Camille had been able to preserve, and I would like to put it around her neck before she leaves us." This final loving gesture shows the artist's undimmed affection for the companion of his early years.

On 26 September a distraught Monet wrote to Pissarro: "You, more than anyone, will understand my grief. I am overwhelmed; I have no idea which way to turn, nor how I am going to be able to organize my life with my two children. I am much to be pitied."

That autumn, probably on account of the bad weather, he abandoned outside work and concentrated on compositions of fruit and flowers; the hunting season inspired some fine still lifes of dead game. The decision to paint still lifes following Camille's death may also have resulted from pressing financial worries, for Monet and his sons were now threatened with eviction, and still lifes sold for higher prices than his landscapes.

A Hard Winter

In the exceptionally hard winter of 1879–80, the Seine suddenly became Monet's only subject matter. The river froze over almost completely, and a memorable thaw followed, with huge ice floes driven down by the current. This event fascinated the artist, who felt a growing interest in atmospheric phenomena; it also gave him a

*C*amille Monet in 1871 (above).

*C*amille Monet on Her Deathbed (1879, left). This canvas, which is handled like a "snow effect," reveals Monet's concern with color analysis.

"At the deathbed of a woman who had been very dear to me, I surprised myself in the instinctive act of tracing the successions and gradations of color that death had just imposed upon her still face. It was a natural desire to preserve a last image of one about to leave us forever.... But before the idea of capturing those features...even occurred to me, at the deepest level of my being I reacted instinctively to the shocks of their color."

Monet, quoted by Georges Clemenceau, 1928

chance to paint several spectacular compositions, with effects that differed according to the angle of vision and the time of day. Monet would soon not need to move his easel at all, or only very slightly, to allow the shifts in form and color caused by changes in the light to exclude all other subject matter from his work.

His Vétheuil pictures seem to possess a peculiarly emotional dimension. These cold-toned landscapes

"We have had a terrific breakup of ice here, and naturally I have tried to do what I can with it."
Letter to Dr. de Bellio
8 January 1880

are empty of any living thing; sky and water often share the same wintry pallor, silence, and desolation. They reflect the material and moral anxieties that were oppressing Monet. As if by a mysterious "association," such as one might find in the poetry of Charles Baudelaire, nature had united with Monet's private melancholy.

It has been suggested that the Ice Floes should be read as symbolizing the painter's lot at the time: The breaking of the ice illustrates both the breakup of the Impressionist group and the turning point in Monet's private life— for the death of Camille, the model for much of his early work, defined the end of an era.

The Seine fills the entire foreground in *Ice Floes Near Vétheuil* (1880, above): The vertical shapes of the bushes and tree trunks are balanced by their reflections in the water. Monet distinguishes in his brushwork between the moving water and the hard blocks of ice.

A Double Challenge: The Salon and a First Solo Exhibition

Ice Floes on the Seine (1880, below).

Having remained aloof from the Salon since 1870—when the jury had yet again rejected his submissions—Monet decided to take up the official gauntlet one more time in 1880. Renoir's success the year before, with his *Portrait of Mme. Georges Charpentier and Her Children*, may have had something to do with this change of heart.

Knowing that this act would be condemned by the Impressionists as treason, especially since he, Monet, had helped found the movement in 1874, the artist took care to write to Duret explaining that his only motive was to sell paintings.

Only one of his two submissions, *Lavacourt*, was accepted, but was exhibited poorly. Zola criticized Monet's too hastily executed canvases, though he acknowledged his talent and forecast his success: "In ten years, he will be accepted, displayed, and rewarded; he will sell his pictures for huge prices and will stand at the head of the present movement" ("Naturalism at the Salon," III, *Le Voltaire*, 21 June 1880).

At the same time that Monet returned to the Salon he turned his back on the fifth exhibition by the Impressionists—who had called themselves "independent

"Everything shimmers ...this thaw is all a mirage; you see no difference between the ice and the sunshine, and all these floes of ice break up the hues of the sky and sweep them away, and the trees shine so that one cannot tell if their russet color comes from autumn, or from their species, and one no longer knows where one is, nor if this is the bed of a river or a woodland clearing."

Marcel Proust

"For the Salon I had to do something more restrained and bourgeois."

Letter to Duret
8 March 1880

Monet's landscape *Lavacourt* (left) is more a careful description than a personal interpretation of the subject. The fragmented brushwork in the handling of the water is restrained beneath a smooth paint surface. Here he sacrifices "immediacy" to give a more conventional aura to his canvas, which was accepted by the Salon and noticed by Zola (below).

artists" since the previous year. This confirmed the breakup of the group, which had already begun with the defections of Renoir, Sisley, and Cézanne. In June the first private exhibition entirely devoted to Monet was held at the gallery of *La Vie Moderne*, a magazine founded in 1879 by the publisher Georges Charpentier. The catalogue, with a preface by Théodore Duret, included eighteen works. The several sales that followed gave Monet a chance to pay off his creditors and brought him fresh hope and courage. "I am working a lot and am on the right track," he wrote to Duret on 5 July 1880.

In August he took part in the 1880 Exhibition of the Le Havre Friends of the Arts Society. His paintings, including the Salon entry, were ill received in his hometown. On the other hand, the seascapes that he painted on the Normandy coast during the next few years enjoyed more success in Paris.

"I Must Soon Leave Vétheuil, and I Am Looking for a Pretty Place by the Seine. I Have Been Thinking About Poissy" (Letter to Zola, 24 May 1881)

After Camille's death Monet's domestic situation

and that of the Hoschedés became confused; business seems to have kept Ernest in Paris, while Alice stayed with Monet, saying she had to look after his two sons.

The Vétheuil period constitutes a major transitional interlude between Argenteuil and Giverny. At this point Monet's life and career began to move in new directions that were decisive for the

In his painting of Théodore Duret (1868, left) Edouard Manet stresses the elegance of a man he called "the last of the dandies." The work was inspired by the Spanish painter Francisco de Goya, and indeed it was in Madrid that Manet first met Duret, an art critic and a loyal supporter of Monet.

LE PEINTRE

CLAUDE MONET

NOTICE SUR SON ŒUVRE

Par Théodore DURET

SUIVIE DU CATALOGUE DE SES TABLEAUX

Exposés dans la galerie du Journal Illustré

LA VIE MODERNE

7, boulevard des Italiens, 7

LE 7 JUIN 1880 ET JOURS SUIVANTS

future. First, he had reached a mature age and had not only assimilated his previous artistic experiences but also acquired his independence, by detaching himself from the old Impressionist group. Second, with the death of Camille and the growing importance to him of the woman who was later to become his second wife, his private life took a different course. Finally, the sustained support of Durand-Ruel seemed to augur better days to come. All these hopeful signs are marvelously captured in *The Artist's Garden at Vétheuil*, which he painted a few months before his departure. In December 1881 (mostly thanks to Durand-Ruel, who paid for the move) Monet abandoned Vétheuil to move in with Alice

The names of Monet and Duret on the catalogue for Monet's 1880 exhibition. On 8 July Monet wrote to Duret: "I am sending you a souvenir of my exhibition, with which you so courageously assisted me."

The Artist's Garden at Vétheuil (1881). Fragmented brushwork makes the sunflowers shimmer.

Hoschedé and the children at Poissy, about twenty miles to the east, in the Villa Saint-Louis, another house near the river.

Durand-Ruel: A Many-Sided, Effective, and Loyal Supporter

At the beginning of the 1880s the name Georges Petit disappears from the roster of Monet's buyers and is replaced by that of Durand-Ruel, who was to supply the artist with unflagging moral and financial aid thereafter.

As the years went by, Durand-Ruel gained more and more influence, eventually supplanting the old group of patrons (the singer Jean-Baptiste Faure, Duret, Charles Ephrussi, de Bellio, and Murer), to whom Monet now refused to sell his work for low prices. Durand-Ruel's purchases, which came steadily after February 1881, allowed Monet to forsake the Salon entirely and to hold aloof yet again from the Impressionists, who mounted their sixth exhibition in the same year.

Painted on a hillside at Vétheuil, this 1880 picture, *Spring*, records that season in the Seine valley. The canvas, which is bare in some places, is thinly covered with light, bright colors that suggest the limpidity of the air and the evanescent clouds. The tree, which has just begun to bud, reminiscent of the flowering almonds of Japanese prints, conveys the rebirth of nature. After the memorable 1880 winter, Monet welcomes the return of warm weather.

R*ough Sea at Etretat* (1883).

In 1882, however, the collapse of the Banque de l'Union Générale hit Durand-Ruel hard; Monet's reaction was to change his mind and take part in the Seventh Exhibition of Independent Artists to the tune of thirty-five canvases. This exhibition was organized in March at the Panorama de Reichshoffen (251 Rue Saint-Honoré, Paris). Although some journalists, notably Joris-Karl Huysmans in 1880, continued to find fault with the Impressionist vision and with Monet's highly personal use of color, the seascapes he showed were greatly admired.

D*urand-Ruel* (right) photographed in around 1910.

Following a burst of intense creativity at Pourville on the Normandy coast, where he tackled several new subjects, Monet went through a period of uncertainty during the winter and following summer: "The future seems very black. Doubt has overtaken me, I think I'm lost and can do nothing more" (letter to Durand-Ruel, 18 September 1882). With his usual generosity, the dealer, who had become Monet's friend, responded with money and abundant advice; he exhibited canvases by Monet in London and Berlin, and in October bought twenty of the pictures completed in Normandy.

It was also in 1882 that Monet began the decoration of the large drawing room in Durand-Ruel's apartment at 35 Rue de Rome, on which he was to work until 1885. In March 1883 the dealer mounted an exhibition of fifty-six of Monet's paintings in his new gallery in Paris. The indifference of the press and public on this occasion was a heavy blow to Monet, who blamed Durand-Ruel for preparing the exhibition badly.

Each time he sold a painting, Monet made a careful note both of its price and of its buyer; thus under 13 January 1884 (below) he noted the canvases acquired by Durand-Ruel.

"I Am Going to…Find a House and a Landscape That Suit Me" (Letter to Durand-Ruel, 5 April 1883)

On several occasions Monet expressed his aversion "to this wretched Poissy," which inspired him not at all: "The countryside won't do for me," he wrote to Durand-Ruel on 27 May 1882. In effect, his short interlude at Poissy was a failure, his important work that year being mostly done on the Normandy coast. His letters to Alice Hoschedé reveal the growing intimacy between the two at this time: "Remember that I love you and cannot live without you" (Etretat, 12 February 1883).

No doubt the dissatisfaction Monet felt with Poissy helped him to realize his vital need to find a suitable place to work. At the age of forty-two, he now required real stability. Thus began his search through the country to fulfill his longstanding aim, which he reiterated to Durand-Ruel: "Once I get properly installed," he wrote on 5 April 1883, "I shall come to Paris only once a month on dates decided in advance." The year before, he had given up his Paris studio on the Rue de Vintimille.

The move from Poissy was again paid for by Durand-Ruel, and Monet acknowledged that "all this makes a great deal more money that I owe you, but once I am set up I hope to paint masterpieces, because the country here pleases me very much." He had discovered Giverny.

In 1882, with *The Cliffs Near Dieppe* (opposite), Monet conveys the often dramatic rocky seashore precipices of the region. By contrast, the light-filled canvas above evokes the happy atmosphere of a summer *Cliff Walk at Pourville*. The figures (perhaps Alice Hoschedé and one of her daughters) stand out against the sea.

A letter from Monet to Durand-Ruel (left), written from Poissy on 20 December 1881.

" I am in ecstasy. Giverny is splendid country for me," wrote Monet to Duret in 1883. Through all his painting expeditions of the 1880s, the artist never tired of expressing in his letters his growing attachment for this village about forty miles northwest of Paris, at the junction of the Epte and the Seine rivers. Seven years later, "certain of never finding a comparable house nor such beautiful countryside anywhere else," he bought the property at Giverny.

CHAPTER V
"GIVERNY IS SPLENDID COUNTRY FOR ME"

Monet communicated his passion for boating to his new family. In *Boat at Giverny* (c. 1887, detail) he painted the Hoschedé girls (Suzanne, left, and Blanche) fishing on the Epte near the house. Monet in around 1887 (right).

Monet's Discovery of the Mediterranean Coast

No sooner was he established at Giverny in 1883, with Alice Hoschedé and the children, than Monet learned with sadness that his friend Manet had died on 30 April.

In December Monet went for the first time to the Mediterranean coast, along with Renoir; after visiting Cézanne at Aix-en-Provence, the two artists pressed on into Italy, traveling as far as Genoa. Then, in January of the following year, Monet returned to spend three months on the Riviera, staying just over the Italian border "at Bordighera, one of the most beautiful places we have seen on our trip. I hope to bring back a whole series of new things. But I ask you to tell *no one* of this voyage...because I insist on *doing it alone....* I have always worked best in solitude and according to my own impressions" (letter to Durand-Ruel, 12 January 1884).

Bordighera is known for the softness of its climate and the tropical luxuriance of its vegetation. Monet felt that he had found an "earthly paradise": "One can wander indefinitely under the orange trees, lemon trees, and palms, and also beneath the admirable olives. ... I should like to paint orange and lemon trees standing against the blue sea.... As to the blue of the sea and sky, it is impossible" (letter to Alice Hoschedé, 26 January 1884).

To convey the light and atmosphere of the region, Monet used unaccustomed tones, of which he took care to forewarn Durand-Ruel in a letter summing up his stay in Italy: "It may draw howls from the enemies of blue and pink, for it has exactly that brightness and fairy light, and I am determined to catch it. Everything is [colored] pigeon-breast and flaming punch, it

In the foreground of *Villas at Bordighera* (1884, opposite, details and photographs below and far right) is the villa built in 1880 for Baron Bischoffsheim by architect Charles Garnier. To paint the Ligurian landscape, Monet said "one would need a palette of diamonds and gemstones" (letter to Duret, 2 February 1884).

is wonderful, and every day the country is lovelier, and I am enchanted" (11 March 1884).

"Rounded Like a New Moon, the Little Town of Etretat, with Its White Cliffs, Its White Shingle, and Its Blue Sea, Lay in the Sunshine" (Maupassant, *Le Modèle*, 1883)

Between 1883 and 1886, Monet regularly went back to Etretat, north of Le Havre; the picturesqueness of its site seems to have attracted him as much as the sky and sea.

A fellow visitor to this region was the writer Guy de Maupassant, who made it the setting for a great many of his stories. Maupassant shared Monet's admiration, and there are strong links between the exactly contemporary works of the two men, who met several times at Etretat.

"Here I will concentrate on the palm trees and the more exotic features."
Letter to Durand-Ruel
23 January 1884

The cliffs at Etretat and the Porte d'Aval (pencil drawing from a sketchbook, c. 1883, opposite).

Following in the footsteps of Courbet and Boudin, Monet painted the striking rock formations of the Porte d'Amont, the Manneporte, and the Porte d'Aval, sometimes including the Aiguille, a needle-shaped rock. "You can have no idea of the beauty of the sea… as to the cliffs here, they are like nowhere else" (letter to Alice Hoschedé, 3 February 1883).

Figure 52
Caillebotte
Petit 12
Vangogh

de Bellio

Spring 1886: A Few Days in Holland

Monet was fascinated by the fields of tulips between Leiden and Haarlem. He brought home five paintings of them, which he finished in his Giverny studio. Here he treated the sky with a certain lightness, but the size of the space it occupies suggests the broadness of the Dutch skyline without taking precedence over the flowers.

Two versions of this subject appeared on 15 June 1886 in the Fifth International Exhibition of Paintings and Sculptures at the Georges Petit Gallery, where they provoked this comment from Huysmans: "There are fields of tulips in Holland by Claude Monet, which are overwhelming! A true feast for the eyes" (letter to Odilon Redon, 28 June 1886). "Everything in the show was sold for high prices to good people," Monet wrote to Berthe Morisot.

The Hunt for Buyers

Though Durand-Ruel's financial problems worried Monet enough to make him consider abandoning his dealer and selling directly to buyers, he admitted that "because I know how far I have come,

M onet's enthusiasm for Holland comes through in the duke of Treviso's record of his remarks (*Le Pèlerinage de Giverny*, 1927): "You don't like tulip fields? You find them too regular? I love them, and I love it when they gather the old flowers to pile them up, and suddenly on the little canals one sees rafts of colors floating, like yellow stains in the blue mirror of the sky"—an effect that comes across here *(Tulip Fields at Sassenheim Near Haarlem,* opposite below, and details above). The painting is very heavily worked, and the undulation of the tulips in the wind is rendered by rapid brush strokes.

thanks to you,...I am aghast at the thought of going out after buyers all over again" (letter to Durand-Ruel, 18 May 1884).

In his eagerness to dispose of his work, Monet took part in several of the international exhibitions organized annually by Georges Petit. He tried to convince Durand-Ruel that he too would benefit from the success of this rival; in effect, Monet began to divide his work between the two dealers. For example, at the 1886 exhibition by a group of painters called Les Vingt in Brussels, Monet's contributions were lent equally by Petit and Durand-Ruel.

Monet was reticent about Durand-Ruel's American forays on his behalf. "I would like to share your hopes for America," he wrote on 23 January 1886, "but I would prefer, above all, to have my paintings known

T he pages of Monet's address book (center) show the names of friends and collectors, such as Faure, Caillebotte, and de Bellio, and dealers like Theo van Gogh and Georges Petit. It was in Petit's gallery that this version of *Tulip Fields* was exhibited in June 1886.

and sold here." Nonetheless, forty of his canvases appeared at the exhibition Oil Paintings and Pastels by the Paris Impressionists, which was held in New York in 1886. Largely thanks to the support of the American painters Mary Cassatt and John Singer Sargent, this show was a great critical success.

"The Sea Is Completely Beautiful, and as for the Rocks, They Are a Tangle of Extraordinary Coves, Spikes, and Needles" (Letter to Alice Hoschedé, 18 September 1886)

"Yearning to go to Brittany," as he explained in a letter to Berthe Morisot, Monet traveled to Belle-Ile in the Gulf of Morbihan during the autumn of 1886. Here he stayed at a fisherman's house in the village of Kervilahouen, near the western shore of the island, a wild place facing the open

"I am in a superbly wild country, amid a chaos of jagged rocks and a sea filled with unbelievable colors; I am fascinated, though having a deal of trouble, because I was used to painting the Channel and obviously had my own routine, and this ocean is something very different."

Letter to Caillebotte
11 October 1886

Monet's first contact with the Atlantic deeply disconcerted him. He painted several scenes of Belle-Ile, including the spectacular *The "Pyramides" of Port-Coton* (opposite above, and photograph opposite below) and the Bay of Port-Domois with the Roche Guibel. This pierced rock appears on the canvas he gave to Auguste Rodin, *Belle-Ile* (left). The line of the horizon is often placed very high; Monet was intrigued by the incessant struggle between land and sea on this rugged coast, and he made full use of the clash between the rocky masses and the foam-flecked waves.

sea. This part of Belle-Ile inspired about forty paintings, divided into several groups according to the place and the weather.

Here again, it is premature to talk about a series, because with each picture Monet changed his angle of attack. Nevertheless, he was turning over the idea in his mind: "I know that to paint the sea truly, you have to see it every day at all hours and at the same spot, so you get to understand the life of it at that spot; so I do the same subject sometimes four or even six times over" (letter to Alice Hoschedé, 30 October). This period in Brittany gave Monet the chance to employ, though instinctively and unsystematically, a way of approaching his subject matter that he would later develop into a more organized procedure.

At Belle-Ile, Monet met Gustave Geffroy, art critic for the politician Georges Clemenceau's radical newspaper, *La Justice*. Geffroy, who became one of his ardent

"Monet worked in the wind and rain. His easel was anchored with cords and stones."

Gustave Geffroy
Claude Monet, 1924

defenders as well as a close friend, recalled Monet
working in terrible storms, with his easel tied to a cliff.
Monet was also visited by the writer Octave Mirbeau.

"After Wild Belle-Ile, This Will Be Very Soft: There's Nothing Here But Blue, Pink, and Gold" (Letter to Duret, 10 March 1888)

Monet spent the first months of 1888 on the
Mediterranean coast. At Cannes he met Maupassant,
who recommended that he stay at the Château de la
Pinède in Antibes, an artists' hotel where the landscape
painter Henri-Joseph Harpignies was also staying. Here
Monet executed about thirty canvases: "I fence and tussle
with the sun...one should paint here with gold and
gemstones" (letter to Rodin, 1 February 1888)—an
image already suggested by Bordighera. He sometimes
painted the same subject more than once, but these
paintings did not form a true series.

To convey the light of the Mediterranean, Monet used a palette of delicate tones akin to pastels. In this freely painted canvas, *Antibes Seen from the Cap* (left, details above), the brushwork exactly imitates the effect of the mistral, a strong wind of southern France, passing over the vegetation.

In June Monet sold ten of his canvases to Theo van
Gogh, Vincent's brother, who was working for the
dealers Boussod and Valadon (formerly Goupil's). Theo
exhibited the paintings, which journalist Félix Fénéon
described in the *Revue Indépendante* as "Ten Antibes

Seascapes," in the showroom adjoining the gallery (19 Boulevard Montmartre). Though this exhibition pleased neither Fénéon nor Pissarro (who was then preoccupied with Neo-Impressionist theories), it was a great success with Maupassant, Mallarmé, and Geffroy. Berthe Morisot described its impact in a letter to Monet: "You have really won over the public, mulish as it is. The people one sees at Goupil's are full of admiration."

Fortified by the acquisition of a new buyer, Monet refused to take part in the group exhibition that opened

In *Antibes Seen from La Salis* (below and in photograph) Monet paints a panorama of Antibes, "a small fortified place gilded by the sun, which stands out against beautiful blue and pink mountains" (20 January 1888).

on 25 May in the Paris gallery of Durand-Ruel, despite the fact that he still disapproved of the dealer's efforts to promote his work in the United States.

The Valley of the Creuse

"Here I am again grappling with the difficulties of a new landscape. It's superb here, with a terrible wildness that reminds me of Belle-Ile. I thought I would do astonishing things, but the further I go, the more trouble I have in conveying it as I would like" (letter to Morisot, 8 April 1889).

Among the twenty-odd paintings inspired by the Creuse River, in western France, groups of two or three stand out as before; but now for the first time a much more important ensemble appears, which includes no fewer than nine works. After the Ice Floes of Vétheuil, the Dutch Tulip Fields, and the seascapes of Belle-Ile and Antibes, each of which constituted a progressive, unconscious, serial approach to given subjects, it seems that these nine views of the Creuse gorge finally brought the series idea to fruition. The number of versions executed by Monet of a subject viewed from a nearly identical vantage point has suddenly increased; the single most important feature has become the variation of the light. These nine landscapes really deserve to be called a series, a word the artist himself used to describe them: "With this awful gloomy weather...I am terrified when I look at my paintings; they are so dark. Moreover, some of them even lack sky. It's going to be a lugubrious series" (letter to Alice Hoschedé, 4 April 1889).

In a letter dated 24 April, Monet told Geffroy about the trouble he was having painting this landscape, mostly due to the season. "I am continually forced to make changes, I follow nature but cannot catch her, and then

"Monet lingered to contemplate the frothing currents which met beyond the rocks on a pebbled bed...the stony hills formed a dark arena around this watery tumult. It was a savage, infinitely sad spectacle."
Gustave Geffroy
Claude Monet, 1924

In Monet's nine pictures of the junction of the Grande and the Petite Creuse rivers, earth and water share the canvas equally. These works differ mainly in their light effects, which vary with the time of day. The three shown here are of evening: *Creuse Valley at Dusk* (above), *Creuse Valley, Evening Effect* (opposite above), and *Creuse Valley, Sunset* (opposite below). Their daring choice of colors captures the feeling of night beginning to fall on the landscape.

there is this river, the level of which drops and rises, which is one day green, the next yellow, the next nearly dry, and which tomorrow may just as easily be a raging torrent." He wrote to Georges Petit on 21 April: "The main thing for me is to be able to be ready in time." During this period, Monet was thinking constantly about the coming exhibition in Paris, where his paintings would be shown with sculptures by Auguste Rodin.

"They Are the Men Who in This Century Have Most Gloriously and Definitively Personified the Twin Arts of Painting and Sculpture" (Octave Mirbeau, *L'Echo de Paris*, 25 June 1889)

As a great admirer of Rodin, Monet was keen to share an exhibition with this officially recognized artist. *"Nothing but you and me,"* he wrote to Rodin on 28 February 1889. "We could do something fine together." The catalogue included 145 entries for Monet and 36 for Rodin; the preface on Monet was signed by Mirbeau, and Rodin was introduced by Gustave Geffroy. The sculptor was especially concerned about his group *The Burghers of Calais,* which was being shown for the first time; as for Monet, he viewed the affair as a retrospective of twenty-five years of work, with pictures spanning his career between 1864 and 1889. "A résumé of the painterly existence of Claude Monet," wrote Geffroy in *La Justice*, 21 June 1889. In spite of a few criticisms, the reaction of the press was largely favorable.

After the opening of the exhibition on 21 June Monet wrote to Georges Petit: "I saw that my panel at the back is completely lost now that the Rodin group has been set up. The mischief is done; it is very upsetting to me. If Rodin

GALERIE GEORGES PETIT
8, rue de Sèze, 8

CLAUDE MONET

A. RODIN

PARIS
—
1889

Monet had long wished to see his name united with Rodin's; this wish was finally realized on the cover of the catalogue for their 1889 joint exhibition (above). Rodin, c. 1887, and his *The Burghers of Calais* (below).

had understood that since we were exhibiting together we should have agreed on the placement of our work... if he had discussed it with me and given a little consideration to my work, it would have been quite easy to work out a fair arrangement without doing each other harm. I only want one thing now and that is to get back to Giverny and have some peace." An open quarrel between these two great artistic temperaments was only just avoided.

Édouard Manet's renowned *Olympia* (1863) was the focus of Monet's attention in 1889.

Manet's *Olympia*

Also in 1889, three works by Monet had been
shown at the Centennial of French Art, which
opened in May to mark the 1889 Universal
Exposition. Displayed at the same time was
Manet's *Olympia*, which had caused a scandal at
the 1865 Salon. Monet decided to raise money
from friends of Manet to buy his *Olympia* and
donate it to the Louvre. "It's a fine gesture of homage
to his memory, and at the same time a discreet way of

helping out his widow, to whom this painting belongs," he wrote to Rodin on 25 October 1889.

This campaign met with opposition from Antonin Proust, formerly the Minister for Fine Arts. "This Proust is a fine ass," wrote Monet to Morisot on 22 January 1890. "I will tell him as much in a letter, and once war has been declared, we shall fight to the finish." Monet finally succeeded in forcing the State's acceptance of *Olympia* for the Musée du Luxembourg; the painting was not moved to the Louvre until 1907, following Georges Clemenceau's intervention.

Monet now returned to his easel. On 11 July he wrote to Morisot: "This devilish painting is making me sweat blood…. I might have expected as much, after all that time doing nothing."

"I Am Yearning for Giverny"

While he was traveling, Giverny was constantly in Monet's mind. He thought of his garden, of his sons, Jean and Michel, of his mistress, Alice, and of the Hoschedé children. "I shall be happy to come back and resume my life in the country. It seems to me I shall derive deep pleasure from painting there" (letter to Alice,

Several works by Monet show the Hoschedé girls boating on the Epte: *Study of a Boat* from a sketchbook (opposite above), and *Boat at Giverny* (c. 1887, above). The river mirrors the figures. Germaine (standing), Suzanne, and Blanche stand out against the foliage as if in a tapestry.

The vegetation is even more commanding in another canvas created at the same time, from which the sky is once again absent: *The Boat* (opposite). This time the boat, the "Norvégienne," is empty, placed in one corner of the frame to leave more room for the water plants.

"I am working as never before, and at new projects, figures in the open air as I understand them, done like landscapes. It is an old dream that still haunts me."

Letter to Duret
13 August 1887

Both at Vétheuil and in his travels, Monet abandoned figurative work. Around 1885, and for the last time, he attempted human figures in a landscape, handling the theme as a landscapist and Impressionist with particular emphasis on the luminous "envelope" surrounding the model. In 1886 Suzanne Hoschedé appeared in these two versions of *Woman with Parasol Facing Right* (left) and *Woman with Parasol Facing Left* (opposite, above left). Monet here captures the fleeting moment before his eyes. The parasol breaks up the light; the floating scarf, the rippling of the dress, and the bending grass suggest a windy day. The movement of the young woman, whom Monet has made almost featureless, corresponds to that of the clouds behind her. He called these two matching paintings *Sketches of Figures in the Open Air.*

Bordighera, 12 February 1884). Monet's attachment to Giverny shines through in both his letters and his work. In the catalogue for the Monet-Rodin exhibition, Monet chose to group four canvases executed at Giverny (including *In the "Norvégienne")* under the title *Sketches of Figures in the Open Air.* They depicted the Hoschedé girls, whom he called "my pretty models" in a letter to Morisot, 11 July 1890. These "glorious Giverny figures," to use Octave Mirbeau's expression, evoke the ideal world that Monet had created for himself, uniting his private life and his painting.

Mirbeau, who recognized this art of living untrammeled by any sort of artifice, laid special stress in his catalogue preface on Monet's domestic happiness: "Paris, with its fevers, its struggles, its intrigues that sap one's will and destroy one's courage, could not suit a stubborn contemplative such as he, a man whose great passion is the life contained in things. He lives in the country…and the open air is his studio. Here, far from the rumors, the coteries, the juries, the aesthetics, and the ugly jealousies, he is producing some of the loveliest—and most noteworthy —works of our time."

The sight of Suzanne outlined against the sky on a bank at the mouth of the Epte may have reminded Monet of a similar composition of Camille and Jean in 1875 (*The Promenade*, above). In any case, the two 1886 canvases evoke the memory of his dead wife; indeed, the painter seems to have been so moved by the resemblance that he could not bring himself to trace Suzanne's features.

Left: Monet made a drawing after *Woman with Parasol Facing Left* to illustrate an article about himself by Mirbeau (7 March 1891, *L'Art dans les Deux Mondes*).

"I am working doggedly at a series of different effects. The farther I go, the more I realize that I must work very hard if I am to find what I am looking for: I am repelled by easy facility.... I am more and more passionate about the need to convey what I feel, and pray that I might live for a while longer not too sunk in helplessness, because it seems I will yet make progress."

Letter to Gustave Geffroy, 7 October 1890

CHAPTER VI
HAYSTACKS, POPLARS, AND CATHEDRALS: THE SERIES PAINTINGS

In this *Effect of Wind,* from the Poplars series (1891), the trees describe a decorative curve from the upper foreground to the lower background. Monet in 1897 (right).

After the *Olympia* campaign, Monet got back to work. His art now moved in a new direction, which had been in the cards for some time; from this point on he only rarely painted isolated compositions, and the canvases he completed during the last six months of 1890 (Poppy Fields and Haystacks) all show that he was now steadily adhering to the idea of the series.

The Haystacks: A Triumph That Sealed the Reconciliation with Durand-Ruel

With its score or so of versions, the Giverny Haystacks series was the first of its kind. In early 1891 the Boussod-Valadon Gallery bought three canvases from Monet at 3000 francs each. The disagreements of 1888 were now forgotten, and the artist's relations with Durand-Ruel were back on a sound footing. On several occasions Monet wrote asking for money to enable him to complete his purchase of the house and garden at Giverny; on 15 December 1890, no doubt with an eye to his own interests, he confided that "I am keeping some pictures for you, but have not managed to hold on to all of them. Valadon came to see me and bought several,

M onet painted different versions of the poppy fields in the meadows at Les Essarts, not far from his home (*Poppy Fields, Giverny,* 1890–1, above and detail at right). Here Clemenceau saw him working "in pursuit of those distillations of light, which change the look of things from one moment to the next." These poppies recall the canvas painted at Argenteuil in 1873, while the poplars, which blocked the horizon in *Ice Floes* (1880), are now seen in isolation, or else arranged curtainlike in the background.

and I had a lot of trouble retaining the Haystacks."

A letter from Pissarro confirms the instant success of the series. "People want only Monets; it seems he can't paint enough to go around. The most amazing thing is they all want *Haystacks: Evening Effect....* Everything he does goes straight to America at prices of four, five, and six thousand francs" (letter from Pissarro to his son Lucien, 3 April 1891).

In May fifteen versions of the Haystacks were unveiled at Durand-Ruel's gallery, in a show entitled "Recent Works by Claude Monet." The catalogue included a preface by Monet's friend Geffroy.

Pissarro was full of praise: "These paintings seem to me very luminous, undoubtedly the work of a master; the colors are pretty rather than strong, the draftsmanship fine but drifting, particularly in the backgrounds. Nevertheless, he's a very great artist!

"When I saw Monet facing his poppy field with his four canvases, changing his palette to keep pace with the moving sun, I had the impression of one involved in a study of light that grew in precision as his subject, supposedly unchanging, revealed to him a greater and greater degree of luminous mutability. It was an evolution in progress, the development of a new means of contemplation, feeling, and expression: A revolution. Indeed this field of poppies with its three poplars marks the beginning of a new age in our history of sensation and expression."
Georges Clemenceau,
"La Révolution de Cathédrales,"
La Justice, 20 May 1895

Preparatory pencil study for Haystacks (c. 1890).

Haystacks in Winter and Summer...

Having made the decision to purchase the house in which he was living, Monet gave up travel for a while. At the same time, he expressed his love of Giverny with a series of passionate studies of the haystacks around his property: *Haystacks, Late Summer, Morning Effect* (1890–1, opposite above, and details left above) and *Haystacks, Effect of Snow, Morning* (1890–1, opposite below, and details left below). He observed them from different angles, but the quantity and similarity of the compositions allow us to describe them as his first full-fledged series, the more so because all were done with the single purpose of studying the interplay of light and form, for which such haystacks were ideal. Several sub-series may also be distinguished according to the number of haystacks (one or two) or the relationship between two haystacks, which are sometimes separated and sometimes so close together that one obscures the other.

Haystacks, *Effect of Snow, Dull Weather* (1890–1, overleaf).

Claude Monet 9[?]

...and From Dawn till Dusk

Monet wrote to Geffroy on 7 October 1890, while he was painting his *Haystacks, Late Summer, Evening Effect* (opposite above, and details left above): "At this time of year the sun goes down so fast that I can't follow it." Then came *Haystack, Melting Snow, Sunset* (1890–1, opposite below, and details left below). He captured ephemeral effects that vary with the hour of the day, with the weather, and with the seasons from the end of summer through to winter. All the versions of Haystacks reflect the position of the sun at a given instant. This is indicated by the direction and changing length of shadows cast on the ground, and their color, which is often blue or mauve. Monet plays with the light and takes advantage of backlighting.

" Monet, you have so astounded me lately with your Haystacks that I catch myself looking at the fields through the prism of your paintings; or rather they seem to impose themselves upon me in that way.**"**

Mallarmé to Monet
July 1890

"Needless to say it is a huge success, and is all so attractive that frankly I'm not surprised. The pictures breathe contentment" (5 May 1891).

Spring, Summer, and Autumn 1891: Poplars

The next subject for his series method was poplars. Monet was in the habit of mooring his boat on the Ile aux Orties, on the bank of the Epte river above Giverny. It happened that while he was at work the common land of the nearby marsh was put up for auction. Monet, to avert the felling of the poplars before he had finished his paintings, did not hesitate. On 8 October 1891 he produced cash for the timber merchant who had acquired the land.

Like the Haystacks, this series of twenty compositions was an instant success. In January 1892 Maurice Joyant, who had replaced Theo van Gogh at Boussod-Valadon, bought some of the canvases and mounted a small exhibition of them at the Boulevard Montmartre gallery. In March Durand-Ruel showed fifteen versions of the Poplars (he himself had bought seven at 4000 francs apiece). This was the first time that a series had been exhibited as a composite work. The public was enchanted. "I am very pleased with your news of my exhibition," Monet wrote to Durand-Ruel on 22

March. "I have it from several authorities that the effect has been considerable."

In the same letter he once again declined to sell his work only through Durand-Ruel: "I think it absolutely damaging and bad for an artist to sell to one dealer only." And then he makes certain conditions which hint at his newfound wealth. "From now on, I no longer wish to sell my paintings in advance; I want to finish them first, without hurrying, and I want to wait a while before deciding which ones I will sell."

Alice Hoschedé Becomes Madame Monet

The growing importance of Monet's attachment to Alice Hoschedé through the eighties is clear from the daily letters he

Poplars, previously kept in the background of Poppy Fields and sometimes of Haystacks, now became a separate subject for Monet, which he studied in different lights and seasons. For his *Poplars, Three Pink Trees, Autumn* (1891, below, details left and opposite) his palette was predominantly pink. He also played with the winding course of the Epte, edged by the poplars, to execute from his boat a series of rhythmic, decorative compositions built on curving lines and balanced by the straight, vertical tree trunks. All this expresses Monet's sense of space and his skill in the grading of planes. Here the three trees in the foreground are shown both reflected in the river and rising into the sky. Monet uses a vertical format to emphasize their soaring lines and elegant shapes. To Haystacks, which are bound to the earth, he opposes Poplars, which stand against the sky.

> " What fine things, those three arrangements of poplars in the evening; how painterly, and how ornamental."
>
> Letter from Pissarro to Monet, 9 March 1892

wrote to her while on his travels. From Bordighera: "My heart is always, always at Giverny…you and my children are my entire life…there is no happiness for me except with you" (26 January and 1 February 1884). From Antibes: "You have in me a heart that loves you, someone you can always count on" (26 January 1888). And from Fresselines: "Art and yourself are my life, my sole concern" (28 April 1889). One year after the death of Ernest Hoschedé, Monet put an end to the ambiguity that had surrounded his domestic life for a decade by marrying Alice on 16 July 1892. Four days later he gave away his stepdaughter Suzanne Hoschedé at her wedding at the church in Giverny.

The Rouen Cathedral series, from left to right: *The Portal and the Tour Saint-Romain: Morning Effect, Harmony in White; Sun Effect, End of the Day; Morning Sunlight, Harmony in Blue; Symphony in Gray and Pink* (1892–4). The architecture is not studied for itself, but as a vehicle for pictorial research. To suggest the stone of the facade, Monet uses a rough paint surface that catches the light and imitates the shimmering effect of the sun.

"This Devil of a Cathedral—How Hard It Is to Paint!" (Letter to Alice Monet, 22 February 1893)

Monet's series method was finally systematized with his Cathedrals, when he placed his easel opposite the west facade of the cathedral at Rouen. Though all these pictures are dated 1894, they were in fact done in two separate batches, in 1892 and 1893 (in both cases between February and mid-April), painted from three different angles, and then completed at Monet's Giverny studio. The artist's letters to Alice reveal his way of working and his determination to dominate this subject, of which he produced no fewer than thirty versions. "Every day I add something and come unawares on some new aspect that I hadn't been able to see previously. How hard it is, yet it is working out.... I am broken, I cannot work any more and...I had a night filled with bad dreams: The cathedral was collapsing on me, it seemed to be blue or pink or yellow" (3 April 1892).

Fully aware of the value and originality of this series, Monet treated Durand-Ruel to a shameful bout of blackmail, by dealing at the same time with Boussod-Valadon and with Maurice Joyant. He demanded 15,000

The Cathedrals series is the most spectacular demonstration of Monet's will to convey immediacy in his paintings. His many versions of the subject correspond to his growing sensitivity to atmospheric variations. In contrast to Haystacks and Poplars, the cathedral motif is always the same and is viewed from more or less the same angle, which makes the changing forms under different light conditions all the more striking.

Supplement au Journal

Le G

A LA GALERIE

EXPOSITION

francs for each canvas, but finally settled for 12,000. Twenty versions of the Cathedrals were displayed at the exhibition of Monet's recent works at Durand-Ruel's gallery in May 1895. Their importance was not missed by contemporary painters and writers. In his *Journal,* the painter Paul Signac cites "those marvelously executed walls." Pissarro acknowledges the interest of the series: "I find in it that superb unity which I myself have sought for so long" (letter to Lucien Pissarro, 1 June 1895). Among the eulogies that appeared in the press, the one to which Monet himself paid most attention was a long article by Georges Clemenceau, which was published in *La Justice* (20 May 1895) under the impressive title of "La Révolution de Cathédrales."

"Absolutely Astonishing" Snow Effects

For two months during the winter of 1894–5, Monet stayed near the village of Sandviken, about ten miles from what is now Oslo, the capital of Norway. In the midst of this "white immensity," Mount Kolsaas inspired him to undertake another series: "It is impossible to conceive of lovelier effects than there are here. I mean the snow effects, which are absolutely astonishing, but unbelievably difficult" (letter to his stepdaughter Blanche Hoschedé, 1 March 1895). At the end of his stay, Monet was congratulated by several artists, notably the Norwegian landscapist Fritz Thaulow and Prince Eugen of Sweden, himself a painter. In May, alongside the twenty Cathedrals, the Paris public was confronted at Durand-Ruel's by no fewer than eight Norwegian landscapes.

A Series of Scenes from Monet's Youth

At the age of fifty-five, Monet felt impelled to go back to the landscapes of his early life. In the winters of 1896 and 1897 he returned to Normandy. During the second winter he executed ten paintings of a former customs lookout on the clifftop at Petit-Ailly. This served Monet as a "fisherman's house" at Varengeville, according to the title that Monet gave to some of the works in which it appears. The "little house" is shown at different times of

"I went into Durand-Ruel's to gaze at leisure on the studies of Rouen Cathedral that had so delighted me in the Giverny studio, and now I have brought that many-faceted cathedral away with me, without knowing how. I can't get rid of it…it obsesses me. … With twenty canvases of judiciously chosen effects, the painter has let us understand that he could have, indeed should have, done fifty, a hundred, a thousand more, as many paintings as there might be seconds in his life, should his life last as long as that stone monument. Monet's prophetic eye scans the future and guides our visual evolution, rendering our perception of the universe more penetrating and subtle than before."

Georges Clemenceau, "La Révolution de Cathédrales," 1895

day, according to the series principle. On 1 June 1898 an exhibition opened at the Georges Petit Gallery, featuring these Normandy paintings along with some canvases done at Giverny, the Morning on the Seine series.

The works painted at Vétheuil in 1900 also demonstrate Monet's determination to apply a technique he had recently perfected to subjects connected with his past. He continued to work there right up to the exhibition of "Recent Works by Pissarro and a New

Fifteen years after *The Fisherman's House, Varengeville* (1882, top), this *Cliff at Varengeville* (1897) is freely interpreted with an even more luminous palette. Here Monet is clearly moving toward a decorative art that is close to abstract.

Series by Monet (Vétheuil)," which was mounted in February 1902 by the Bernheim-Jeune Gallery—a new dealer for Monet.

"Every Day I Find London More Beautiful to Paint" (Letter to Blanche Hoschedé-Monet, 4 March 1900)

Another pilgrimage to a place he had known in his youth took Monet back to London on three occasions—in autumn 1899, February 1900, and from February to April 1901. Here he pursued an old ambition to "paint some effects of mist on the Thames" (letter to Duret, 25 October 1887). The Houses of Parliament and the Charing Cross and Waterloo bridges captured his attention. The two bridges he painted from his room at the Savoy Hotel, and Parliament from Saint Thomas' Hospital. But what interested Monet most of all was the prospect of painting the effect of fog in the city, what he called "a superb mist" in a letter to Alice, 24 February 1900.

Faithful to his chosen method, Monet finished

his hundred-odd London paintings in his Giverny studio, and repeated the experience pioneered by his Poplars; thirty-seven of these canvases were exhibited on their own at Durand-Ruel's gallery in May and June 1904 under the title of "Series of Views of the Thames at London (from 1900 to 1904)." The Thames, in fact, constitutes the link between his three sub-series of London motifs.

"I Am Lost in Admiration for Venice" (Letter to Durand-Ruel, 19 October 1908)

After this temporary bout with nostalgia, Monet turned once again to new landscapes. From October to December 1908 (he was now sixty-eight) he took Alice on the last major journey of his life—to

In *The Houses of Parliament: Sun Shining Through a Gap in the Fog* (opposite) and *The Houses of Parliament: Stormy Sky* (above), both completed in 1904, Monet took great liberties with his subject by flattening, narrowing, and vertically elongating the Neo Gothic architecture; the building rises up like a phantom. The tones recall *Impression, Sunrise,* and the atmosphere evokes the visions of J. M. W. Turner and James Abbott McNeill Whistler.

List made out by Monet for his 1904 exhibition at Durand-Ruel's gallery (center).

Venice, the city of painters par excellence. As in London, he continued his struggle to marry architecture, water, and light; the stone of the buildings—in this case, the palaces—was sacrificed to the study of "this unique light" (letter to Geffroy, 7 December 1908). Seeming to care nothing for Venice's venerable past, Monet concentrated on its "magical, fairylike aspect." For this reason his canvases have been compared to the timeless Venice evoked by Marcel Proust in *Remembrance of Things Past:* "We watched the double row of palaces between which we passed reflect the light and angle of the sun upon their rosy surfaces, and alter with them" (*The Sweet Cheat Gone*).

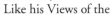

Like his Views of the Thames, Monet's Venetian canvases were completed at Giverny in the years that followed. In May and June 1912 the Bernheim-Jeune Gallery presented twenty-nine Views of Venice divided into several groups (the Grand Canal, San Giorgio Maggiore, and various palaces). At the same time an illustrated album entitled *The Venice of Claude Monet* was published, with an essay by Mirbeau. On 31 May Paul Signac voiced his admiration to the painter: "These Venice pictures, in which everything unites as the expression of your will, in which no detail runs counter to emotion...I admire them as the highest incarnation of your art."

*T*he Doges' Palace *Seen from San Giorgio Maggiore* (1908) illustrates Monet's sense of space: In the foreground, the quay of the island of San Giorgio projects into the lagoon, while the facades of Venice rise from the very surface of the water. Above left: Pencil sketch of the Palazzo Dario.

CLAUDE MONET

"Venise"

Neuf reproductions de Tableaux
(en fac-similé et huit phototypies)
Avec une Préface
par
OCTAVE MIRBEAU

BERNHEIM-JEUNE & Cⁱᵉ
Experts près la Cour d'Appel
15, Rue Richepanse
27, Boulevard de la Madeleine
15, Avenue de l'Opéra
PARIS

"I Pine for Giverny. Everything Must Be So Beautiful There in This Glorious Weather" (Letter to Alice, Rouen, 13 April 1892)

Throughout these years, and during all his travels, Monet never stopped thinking of

Giverny. As the owner of the house since 1890, he had made the garden more beautiful each year, mingling his love for it with his love for his art and his family, particularly Alice. He sent home various plants from the Rouen botanical gardens and promised to bring his children "some plant specimens" from the Nordic lands.

He often dispatched recommendations about flowers to Alice; from Pourville he wrote to her that he dreamed of what he would do at Giverny when the garden was in flower (18 March 1896).

At the end of his life, Monet hardly set foot outside Giverny; it became his sole source of inspiration.

"My enthusiasm for Venice continues to grow, and it saddens me that the moment is coming when I must leave this unique light. It's so beautiful. But I have had delicious moments here, almost forgetting that I am the old man that I am."

Letter to
Gustave Geffroy,
7 December 1908

"Here and there, on the surface, there floated, blushing like a strawberry, the scarlet heart of a lily set in a ring of white petals…a little further on, were others pressed close together in a floating flower bed, as though pansies had flown out of a garden like butterflies and were hovering with blue and burnished wings over the transparent shadowiness of this watery border; this skylike border…"

Marcel Proust, *Swann's Way*, 1913

CHAPTER VII
WATER LILIES: MONET'S FINAL MESSAGE

A flow of light illuminates the lily pads in *Water Lilies— Water Landscape* (1907, left). At right, Monet photographed in around 1920 by playwright Sacha Guitry.

A Pool "With a View to Growing Aquatic Plants, a Thing of Pleasure, to Delight the Eyes, and Also a Source of Subjects for Painting"

After 1890 Monet built himself a new studio. While continuing to lay out his flower garden, he created a second space, which he called his *jardin d'eau,* or water garden. This broad pool, crossed by a bridge, is a reminder of the painter's interest in Japanese art. Though it emerged in Monet's paintings as early as 1895, he focused on it from 1898 through 1900. As in his contemporary Views of Vétheuil, the format for these different compositions is nearly square.

Monet entitled these paintings Nymphéas—the scientific name for the variety of white water lily that he grew in Giverny, and to which in 1885 Mallarmé dedicated a prose poem. Monet returned to the theme of his Japanese bridge in the 1920s, but by that time its airy lightness had been obscured beneath a mass of vegetation and hanging wisteria.

At the end of 1900, twenty-five recent works of Monet

Among the ten or so versions of the Water Lily Pool exhibited at Durand-Ruel's gallery in 1900 was this *Harmony in Pink* (above left; above, detail from a c. 1917 autochrome by Etienne Clémentel —autochrome was a color photographic process invented by the Lumière brothers). The background of the painting is filled by willows, against which the bridge (perhaps inspired by Japanese prints) stands out boldly. Then the artist lowers his eyes to concentrate on the water surface, as in his *Water Lilies* painted in 1907 (opposite below).

"I have to work and would wish to paint everything before my sight goes."

Letter to
Joseph Durand-Ruel,
7 July 1922

With the onset of cataracts, Monet felt a feverish compulsion to record the world of Giverny. His perception of color was altered, and the canvases are hard to date just before or after his eye operations. *The Japanese Bridge* (c. 1923, left) shows the upper arch covered by the wisteria he loved.

were exhibited at the Durand-Ruel Gallery; almost half were versions of the Water Lily Pool.

"The Water Lilies, a Series of Water Landscapes"

This was the title chosen by Monet himself for the 1909 Durand-Ruel exhibition of forty-eight of his works painted between 1903 and 1908: an "out-of-the-ordinary exhibition," in the painter's own words to his dealer (28 January 1909). After 1904 the landscape surrounding the pool is reduced in Monet's paintings to a narrow strip in the upper area of the canvas, and then it gradually disappears altogether, leaving the flowers to occupy the whole frame. "You should know I am immersed in work. These landscapes of water and reflection have become my obsession. It is beyond my old man's strength, yet I still want to convey what I feel. I have destroyed some...but then I start again afresh" (letter to Geffroy, 11 August 1908).

Monet's 1909 exhibition was a great success, hailed by France's most

"A word to let you know the wisteria is nearly out, in a few days it will be splendid, you must come."

Letter to Clemenceau
16 May 1922

Les Nymphéas
Paysages d'eau

prominent critics, including Geffroy, Romain Rolland, Remy de Gourmont, Lucien Descaves, and Roger Marx.

Official Success and Recognition

1903. —	Nᵒ 1.
érie 1904. —	5 Tableaux. Nᵒˢ 2 à 6.
érie 1905. —	7 Tableaux. Nᵒˢ 7 à 13.
érie 1906. —	5 Tableaux. Nᵒˢ 14 à 18.
érie 1907. —	21 Tableaux. Nᵒˢ 19 à 39.
érie 1908. —	9 Tableaux. Nᵒˢ 40 à 48.

After this time, Monet's works appeared in many exhibitions abroad, in Brussels (at the Libre Esthétique gallery), London, Berlin, Stockholm, Dresden, Venice, and of course in the United States, where, thanks to Durand-Ruel, painter Theodore Robinson, and collector Mrs. Potter Palmer, Monet's reputation was firmly established. At the same time Giverny became a shrine for foreign visitors, among them Japanese, Russians (the collector Sergei Shchukin), and Americans (John Singer Sargent, Robinson, and the young student Lilla Cabot Perry, who later wrote an account of her interviews with the master).

In addition to his old friends (Sisley, Pissarro, Morisot, Mallarmé, Rodin, Renoir, and even Cézanne) and his intimates (Geffroy, Mirbeau, and Clemenceau), many new French admirers came to Giverny as well: painters Jacques-Emile Blanche and Pierre Bonnard, Sacha Guitry, publisher Paul Gallimard, and various members of the Goncourt Academy. Finally, however, his antipathy to receiving journalists—a few meetings were granted to François Thiébault-Sisson—and his "great age" led Monet to prefer work and solitude to inconvenient visitors, and to reserve his rare moments of repose for a small group of old friends.

Monet's self-portrait (1917) was done with touches of juxtaposed color. He gave it to Clemenceau, who presented it to the Louvre in 1927.

"Here is the address of the rose-grower...also the names of the roses you noticed. The climber on the front of the house is *Crimson Rambler* and the standard is *Virago.*"
Letter to G. and J. Bernheim-Jeune, 2 July 1909

Meanwhile Durand-Ruel, aided by his sons and still unable to obtain exclusive rights to Monet's paintings, was forced to reach an agreement with the Bernheim-Jeune brothers, who were also regular visitors to Giverny, to buy and exhibit Monet's works. The prices were now enormous (40,000 to 50,000 francs for certain canvases in 1924); the artist himself was stunned by the sums they were fetching.

The time had clearly come for official recognition. Eight paintings from the Caillebotte collection entered the Musée du Luxembourg in Paris in 1896. These were joined in 1906 by works from the Moreau Nélaton collection, in 1907 by *Rouen Cathedral, Harmony in Brown,* and in 1921 by *Women in the Garden*—the same work that had been rejected by the Salon over fifty years before. The latter two paintings were bought directly by the French government, and all were moved to the Louvre a few years later. Monet was also represented in several provincial museums in France and, of course, in many major museums in other countries.

M onet's sketch and list of flowers show his interest in flowers, which he ordered from the growers Truffaut and Vilmorin. He was an avid reader of gardening magazines.

"Water, Lilies, Plants, but Spread over a Wide Surface" (Letter to Raymond Köchlin, 15 January 1915)

During the First World War Monet built himself a top-lit studio, so as to work on his *Grandes Décorations de Nymphéas.* Just after the 1918 armistice he proposed to Clemenceau the gift of two panels to the State, in celebration of France's victory. After lengthy discussions, an act of donation was signed on 12 April 1922, which

"I am currently very busy with my gardeners, with major works in view."

Letter to the ophthalmologist Dr. Coutela, 13 October 1923

established that eight compositions would be hung in the two galleries of the Orangerie in the Tuileries gardens in Paris. The works were to be painted specifically to fit the galleries' oval shape.

In the years that followed, Clemenceau offered Monet tireless encouragement, though the artist was frequently tempted to give up this huge enterprise because he feared the loss of what was most precious to him—his sight. He was suffering from cataracts, and he refused to be operated on until January 1923, fearing that an operation might rob him of his sight altogether.

"How Terrible It Is to Reach the End of One's Life"

This observation, made in a letter from Monet to Geffroy on 7 February 1899 just after the deaths of Sisley and Suzanne Hoschedé-Butler (*Woman with Parasol),* was to become a constant refrain in his correspondence, as the painter saw his old friends disappearing one by one: Morisot (1895), Mallarmé (1898), Pissarro (1903), Mirbeau and Degas (1917), and Renoir (1919—"now I am the last survivor of the group," wrote Monet sadly on 8 December); then Durand-Ruel (1922) and Geffroy (1926). Above all, Monet grieved for his "adored companion" of over thirty years, Alice, who died in

Monet posed for this photograph in front of *Morning* in the early 1920s. Palette and brush in hand, he stands in his last studio, which was specially built for his work on the *Grandes. Décorations,* later housed in the Orangerie. At this time Monet's life at Giverny was entirely governed by the daylight; he received visitors only when he was unable to work in the studio.

"I am well, though very old, and I have my sight back at last, to my great joy. So I have worked joyfully all summer, with more zeal than ever."

Letter to painter
Paul César Helleu,
29 October 1925

1911, and his elder son, Jean, in 1914.

"What a sad end for me," he had written to Geffroy in 1919. But then, after his operation, he partly regained his sight and sought consolation in his work: "I am working as never before, I am happy with what I am doing, and if the new glasses are better still, I ask only to live until I'm a hundred" (letter to André Barbier, 17 July 1925).

Watched over by the woman Clemenceau once called "the angel," Blanche Hoschedé-Monet (his stepdaughter and the widow of his son Jean), Monet died on 5 December 1926 at the age of eighty-six.

Because he had refused to deliver the *Grandes Décorations* during his lifetime, they were now placed in the Orangerie in accordance with his will; the unveiling took place on 17 May 1927. The complete ensemble of Water Lilies represents the final message of the master of Giverny, who expressed himself in a form so innovative as to be close to abstract. Through this legacy, the painter who had led the Impressionists showed himself to be a true man of the 20th century.

In his last years Monet told Clemenceau, "I merely apply my effort to a maximum of appearances, in close correlation to unknown realities. When one is on the plane of concordant appearances, one cannot be too far from reality, or at least from what we are capable of knowing about it. I have done nothing but look at what the universe has shown to me, so as to bear witness to it with my brush."

Overleaf: *Morning, No. 1* and *The Clouds* in the Orangerie.

DOCUMENTS

Monet and the Artists of His Time

Monet's long life is amply documented by a correspondence that reveals his character and places him squarely in the context of his own era. He formed deep relationships free of affectation with his friends, and he applied the same rule to fellow artists, through mutual gifts of paintings, messages of congratulation, and exchanges of views about contemporaries' talents. Sometimes both sides of a correspondence have survived, so that we have in effect dialogues between Monet and his friends.

Monet and Daubigny

At the 1859 Salon the young Monet admired the works of the painters Constant Troyon and Charles-François Daubigny. Daubigny would later introduce Monet to Durand-Ruel in London (1870–1).

Everything you have heard said of Daubigny and me is true, and I have reason to be very grateful to him. When he met me in London during the Commune, I was in serious straits; he was enthusiastic about some of my Thames studies, and he put me in touch with Monsieur Durand-Ruel, thereby saving me and several of my friends from dying of hunger. Help like that one doesn't forget.

Another thing since that time has affected me deeply: Daubigny's purchase of one of my Holland paintings at Durand-Ruel's. But most to his credit is the fact that he resigned as a member of the jury of the official Salon of the time, because it had so unjustly refused work by me and my friends.

Monet to Etienne Moreau-Nélaton
Giverny, 14 January 1925

Entries from Monet's address book.

Monet and Boudin

Eugène Boudin, whom Monet called the "King of the Skies," was his first master—the second was Jongkind. Monet always acknowledged his deep debt to Boudin.

The only good painter of seascapes we have, Jongkind, has died for art. His is a worthy place for you to fill.... I hope you won't refuse me a little sketch of yours as a souvenir, and as to your advice, you know how much attention I pay to it.

Monet to Boudin
Paris, 20 February 1860

We were talking of Monet.... At a dealer's on the Rue Lafayette, there is a view of Paris by him which would be worthy of the great masters, if the details were on a par with the ensemble. That boy has what it takes.

Boudin to F. ("Père") Martin
Paris, 18 January 1869

You write to inform me of your marriage. Will you allow me to send these few lines in happy remembrance of time past? But first of all I want to congratulate you and Madame Monet, whom I had the pleasure of meeting in earlier days, when she entertained us artists so graciously and kindly.

For years now the hazards and necessities of life have kept us apart, but nonetheless I have shared in your efforts and your successes;...with interest I have followed you in your bold endeavors, even in your foolhardy ones, and watched them bring you fame and reputation. The times are long gone when we sallied forth to try our skills at landscape in the Rouelles valley, or along the coast of Sainte-Adresse, or at Trouville and Honfleur—with Jongkind, our good, great, and much-mourned friend.

As I grow older I have but one regret, which is that among the souvenirs I have carefully kept for myself, I have not the smallest painting by you.... You who should be there on my wall to remind me of those early years, which I have to say were times of struggle, hardship, and discouragement.

You owe me this souvenir.... I do not ask it of you for the purely mercenary reason that your paintings have increased in value.

Do as you think fit, my dear Monet, but believe that you would give me the greatest pleasure by remembering this. You have taken possession of your destiny. You have outlived struggle and difficulty. Do this soon, for I grow older with every day that passes.

Boudin to Monet
Deauville, 28 July 1892

I was very touched and very flattered by your request. I am determined to give you something that will be worthy of you.

You know the affection I have always cherished for you, and the gratitude. I have not forgotten that you were the one who first taught me to see and to understand what I saw.

Like you, I have often thought of those early days and of those delightful rambles with Jongkind and Courbet. So I am very happy that you have not forgotten either.

I very much hope to come and shake your hand this winter, and talk again of those good old times.

Your old friend.

Monet to Boudin
Giverny, 22 August 1892

Monet and Bazille

Bazille was the great friend of Monet's youth. Their bond was shattered by Bazille's death in 1870.

I have spent eight days at the little village of Chailly, near the forest of Fontainebleau. I was with my friend Monet, from Le Havre, who is rather good at landscapes. He gave me some tips that have helped me a lot.

Bazille to his mother
1863

Maître Courbet paid us a visit to see Monet's *Picnic*, which delighted him. In fact, over twenty painters have come to see it, and all of them admire it greatly, although it is far from finished (naturally I say nothing of my own work). This painting is bound to cause a furor at the Exhibition.

Bazille to his brother Marc
December 1865

At the moment we are all signing a petition demanding an exhibition of the paintings rejected by the Salon. The petition is supported by every Paris painter who is any good. However, it will come to nothing…so we have decided to rent a big studio each year in which we will exhibit our work. We will invite all the painters we like to send in paintings. Courbet, Corot, Diaz, Daubigny, and plenty more have promised to send things, and very much approve of our idea. With them and Monet, who is the best of all, we are certain of success. You'll see, people will be talking of us.

Bazille to his mother
1867

Frédéric Bazille.

I know better than anyone the true value of the painting [*Women in the Garden*] that I have bought from you, and I very much regret not being rich enough to pay you more for it.

Bazille to Monet
2 January 1868

Monet and Manet

Although he preferred to exhibit his work at the 1874 Salon rather than join the First Impressionist Exhibition, Manet was very close to Monet, to whom he often gave financial assistance. By putting himself at the head of the drive organized to buy Olympia *for the Musée du Luxembourg in 1890, Monet showed his loyalty to his old friend.*

My dear Manet,
I often think of you and of how much I owe you, and it is really most

Edouard Manet.

kind not to have asked for that money back, which you must badly need....

I am very glad to hear that your paintings are so successful. Apparently you have done some marvelous things.

Monet to Manet
Vétheuil, 14 May 1879

I have this minute heard the terrible news that poor Manet is dead. His brother can count on me as a pallbearer. I must go to Paris tomorrow and have a black suit made.

Monet to Durand-Ruel
Giverny, 1 May 1883

Yes, poor Manet was very fond of me, but we return that fondness in equal measure, and I am exasperated by the silence and unjustness being shown by all, about his memory and his great talent.

Monet to Mallarmé
19 June 1888

Monsieur le Ministre,

In the name of a group of subscribers, I have the honor to present to the State *Olympia* by Edouard Manet.

We are convinced that in this we speak for and represent many other artists, writers, and art lovers who have long since acknowledged the important place in this century's history that belongs to this painter, who has been so prematurely lost to his art and his country. In the view of the vast majority of those who take an interest in French painting, the role of Edouard Manet has been both positive and decisive. He not only played a vital individual role; he was also the personification of a great and fruitful development in our art.

It seems to us preposterous that a life's work of such importance has still found no place in our national collections, that the master has not gained entry where his disciples are already well established. Moreover, we view with disquiet the incessant shiftings of the art market, the growing competition from America in the purchasing of our work, and the departure, so easily avoidable, of so many works of art that should be the joy and glory of France. Our wish is to preserve for the nation one of Edouard Manet's most characteristic works, in which he appears in the fullness of triumph, a master of his vision and his art.

We therefore entrust *Olympia* to your care, Monsieur le Ministre. It is our desire to see it take its rightful place in the Louvre, among its contemporaries of the French School. Should regulations stand in the way of its immediate entry, we believe that the Musée du Luxembourg is the obvious choice to receive *Olympia*, and to keep it until the question can be reconsidered.

Monet to Armand Fallières
7 February 1890

Monet and Morisot

Monet admired Berthe Morisot, who was married to Manet's brother Eugène, as both a woman and an artist—she was the leading female Impressionist.

I am far from Paris. I cannot come to admire your work at Petit's; but nearly every day I have letters telling of your successes, and I want to congratulate you on the fact. I have a bow window here overlooking the sea, and a garden that is one great sunburst of flowers. You would do wonders with it!

Morisot to Monet
Jersey, June 1886

It is very kind of you to worry about me, but the truth is that bad weather and age are the only causes of my infirmities. I have become a wheezing old lady. You are charmingly modest, but I know you are in brilliant form and are doing some delightful things.

Berthe Morisot photographed in her studio.

We often talk of you with Mallarmé, who is one of our faithful friends, and a great friend to you too.

Morisot to Monet
14 March 1888

You must think me very forgetful. I wanted to come and see you, and to tell you how lovely I thought your paintings at Durand's were, but I have been very busy here, only coming to Paris for an hour or two; and also I hoped, hearing you were with Mallarmé, that you would come to Giverny.

Have the Goupils at least informed you that they are exhibiting the ten paintings I sold to them? I would be glad to know what you feel about them.

Monet to Morisot
Giverny, early June 1888

Thank you for your kind letter, and for the kind things you say about my wretched paintings at Durand's. I am all the more touched because the show, as you know, is a complete flop.

You have really won over the public, mulish as it is. The people one sees at Goupil's are full of admiration, and I think it rather brazen of you to ask my impression of the show: You know perfectly well it's stunning.

I saw Mallarmé on Thursday. I should be amazed if that charming man doesn't send you a fine letter to express his admiration. We are both very much inclined to come and see you at Giverny.

Morisot to Monet
June 1888

I deeply regret not having seen her one last time before I left [Morisot died in March 1895], and it is a great grief

to me to think she is no more; she was so intelligent, so talented....
It is really very, very sad and hard to see all one's friends dying so soon. Alas, how many of our little group remain today?

Monet to Alice Monet
Sandviken, 10 March 1895

Monet and Cézanne

In his bedroom at Giverny Monet had several paintings by Cézanne. Even the painter who wanted to "go beyond

Cézanne with his painting *The Bathers*.

Impressionism" was forced to acknowledge the superiority of Monet's eye.

I agree to Wednesday. [Monet had invited Geffroy to Giverny to meet Cézanne at a lunch on 28 November 1894. The other guests were Mirbeau, Rodin, and Clemenceau.]

I hope Cézanne will still be here and will join us, but he is so cranky and so shy of new faces that I am afraid he will be absent, despite the yearning he has to meet you. What a shame it is that he has not had more support in his life! He is a real artist, but one who doubts himself overmuch. He needed his spirits raised, so he was most receptive to your article!

Monet to Geffroy
Giverny, 23 November 1894

I want to tell you how glad I was of the moral support you gave me, which still serves to encourage me in my painting.

Cézanne to Monet
Aix, 6 July 1895

I am pursuing success through work. I distrust all living painters save Monet and Renoir.

Cézanne to Joachim Gasquet
Aix, 8 July 1902

I thought I told you during our talk that Monet was living at Giverny; I hope the artistic influence of this master will not fail to influence his entourage directly or indirectly and will produce the necessary effect that it can and must have on a young artist who is eager to work.

Should you meet the master [Monet] whom we both so much admire, remember me to him. I don't think he cares much to be disturbed, but if you show sincerity he may unbend a little.

Cézanne to Charles Camoin
Aix, 13 September 1903

Pissarro on Monet's Work

Though his temporary adherence to Neo-Impressionism led him to criticize Monet's work, Pissarro immediately understood the value of the series paintings of the 1890s.

Pissarro, self-portrait.

He [the critic Braquemond] also noticed the coarse execution of some Monets, for instance a Dutch canvas [a version of Tulip Fields (Stedelijk Museum, Amsterdam) exhibited at the Sixth International Exhibition, at the Georges Petit Gallery, 1887] in which the paint is so thick that it adds an artificial light to that of the picture itself (you cannot conceive how unpleasant I find this) and what is more, allied with a thin, swept-over sky; no, I cannot go along with his approach to art.

Pissarro to his son Lucien
15 May 1887

I told you that what I saw of Monet's pictures did not appear to indicate progress; this view is more or less unanimous among the painters. Degas was one of the harshest critics; he considers them no more than commercial art. Moreover, he has always taken the view that Monet does nothing but fine decorations. But as Fénéon says, it's more vulgar than ever. Renoir thinks it a step backward and so does Durand's son, though it is true he is a rival dealer.

I met Monet at Durand's. I don't know, but he always seems a bit supercilious, I was reading an article in which he was criticized very foolishly, and for such stupid reasons that I brought it to his attention; there was equally stupid praise, too. We didn't speak of painting otherwise—there was no use, he wouldn't have understood me. After all, he may be right; each man must follow his own line as best he can!

Pissarro to his son Lucien
Paris, 10 July 1888

Yesterday Monet's exhibition [which included fifteen versions of *Haystacks*] opened at Durand's. I went with one eye bandaged, so I saw Monet's marvelous *Sunsets* with only one eye.

They seemed to me filled with light, undoubtedly the work of a master. But since, for our own instruction, we must go beneath the surface, I

asked myself what could be lacking. It's hard to make this out; the lack is certainly not one of exactness or harmony, more of execution, of a calmer, less ephemeral way of seeing. The colors are pretty rather than strong, the draftsmanship fine but drifting, particularly in the backgrounds. Nevertheless he's a very great artist!

Of course it is a huge success, and so attractive that frankly I'm not surprised. The pictures breathe contentment. Mirbeau told me about your woodcuts, which he thinks very good, and so does Monet.

Pissarro to his son Lucien
Paris, 5 May 1891

I would be sorry if you did not get here before Monet's exhibition closes; his Cathedrals are going to be dispersed all over the place, and they should really be seen all together. The younger painters, and even some of Monet's admirers, bitterly oppose them. I am intrigued by his extraordinary mastery. Cézanne, whom I met yesterday at Durand's, agrees that it is the work of a determined, level-headed man, pursuing elusive effects and nuances that no other artist we know can match. Some artists think such research unnecessary; personally I think any research is justifiable if it is as deeply felt as this.

Pissarro to his son Lucien
Paris, 26 May 1895

You remember that Monet's Cathedrals were all done with a heavily veiled effect, which lent the monument a certain mysterious charm.

Pissarro to his son Lucien
Rouen, 24 March 1896

Monet in the garden at Giverny.

Monet and Caillebotte

Monet and Caillebotte were united by their passions for painting and gardening. It was due to Caillebotte's 1894 bequest that eight canvases by Monet entered the Musée du Luxembourg in 1896.

My dear friend,

Be sure and come on Monday, as we agreed, for all my irises will be in flower; any later and some of them will be over. Here is the name of the Japanese plant which is coming to me from Belgium: *Crythrochaete*. Try to speak to M. Godefroy about it and give me some clues as to how I can best look after it.

Monet to Caillebotte
Giverny (undated)

My dear Martial,

I received the photographs of Gustave this morning, and they have given me great pleasure. Thank you so much for them and for having thought to send me the one of you both together.

I hope that everything is arranged with the [Ecole des] Beaux-Arts, and that they will now take possession of the pictures which are to be hung at the Luxembourg.

When you reach the stage of organizing and hanging the exhibition, don't hesitate to let me know and make free use of me. You know how happy I am to do something for his memory.

Monet to Martial Caillebotte
(Gustave's brother), 22 May 1894

Monet and Sisley

Alfred Sisley commended his children to Monet's care just before his death.

Poor Sisley asked to see me eight days ago, and I saw quite clearly that he was bidding me farewell. Poor old friend, poor children!

Monet to Geffroy
29 January 1899

My dear friend,

I am currently arranging a sale to help Sisley's two children, who have been left penniless, and since their father has bequeathed them very few paintings from his studio, we are to contribute some pictures by his friends and colleagues to the sale of his work, which should raise the funds his poor children need. Naturally I am assured of the cooperation of everyone who took part in our early exhibitions, and I thought that if your mother had been alive she would have been glad to join us in this good deed; if you find you have one of her paintings you can bear to part with, to do so would be a homage to her, which would associate both her and you with an act of kindness. As for us, we shall give the best of what we have, so the sale can successfully raise some money for the Sisley children.

Monet to Julie Manet, daughter of
Berthe Morisot and Eugène Manet,
Giverny, 23 March 1899

Monet and Renoir

As young men Monet and Renoir often worked at their easels side by side. Monet was deeply affected by the illness and death of his friend.

I am at my parents' house, and am nearly always at Monet's. We don't eat every day. Nonetheless I am happy, because Monet is very good company for painting.

Renoir to Bazille
Louveciennes
Summer 1869

Do you want to know the state I am in and how I have been living for the last week? Ask Renoir, who brought us some bread from his home, to keep us from dying of hunger.

Monet to Bazille
Saint-Michel (Bougival)
9 August 1869

Congratulations on the article about the Renoir portrait. Yes, that man is a beautiful and rare painter.

Monet to Geffroy
Giverny, 6 July 1912

You will have guessed that Renoir's death has been a great sorrow to me; he

Renoir painted by Bazille (1867).

has taken with him a part of my life. These last three days I have thought over and over again about our early years of struggle and hope.... It is hard to carry on alone, though it certainly won't be for long: Every day I feel age gaining on me, though people say otherwise.

Monet to Felix Fénéon
mid-December 1919

Monet and Degas

Degas did not always like or understand Monet's work, which he saw as "commercial," or as the product of a "decorative talent." Still, their friendship survived. When he was almost blind, Degas did not hesitate to travel down to Giverny for Alice Monet's funeral in 1911.

I have just had a letter from the Bernheims asking me to intervene with Degas' brother on their behalf, so they can assist you with the public auction. Even though I don't know Degas' brother, my admiration for Edgar's talent, our friendship as young men, and our shared struggle would permit me to write to him on the subject.

Monet to Joseph Durand-Ruel
Giverny, 15 October 1917

Monet and Vincent van Gogh

Van Gogh often referred to Monet's art in his letters. He was keenly interested in the Monet-Rodin exhibition, the catalogue of which was sent to him by his brother Theo.

There are many things to see here.... In Antwerp, I never even knew what the Impressionists were; now I have seen them, and although I am not yet one of their club, I am a great admirer

of some of their paintings... [notably] a landscape by Claude Monet.

Van Gogh to H. M. Levens
Paris, summer or autumn 1886

At the moment my brother is mounting an exhibition of Claude Monet. I would very much like to see it. Guy de Maupassant went there, among others.

Van Gogh to Emile Bernard
Arles, June 1888

You will do something like Durand-Ruel, who recognized the personality of Claude Monet before the others, and bought his paintings.

Van Gogh to his brother Theo
10 September 1888

Oh, to paint figures as Claude Monet paints landscapes! In spite of everything, that is what remains to be done, before Monet comes to be seen as the only Impressionist.

Van Gogh to Theo
May 1889

Monet and Signac

Written on the occasion of Monet's Venice exhibition at the Bernheim-Jeune Gallery in 1912, this splendid exchange of letters between Monet and the Post-Impressionist painter Paul Signac reveals their mutual respect.

Dear Master,
Confronted with your Venice paintings, such admirable renderings of subjects I know so well, I felt an emotion as complete and strong as that which I had felt in about 1879, in the *Vie Moderne* exhibition room, before your paintings of the Gare Saint-Lazare and Rue Montorgueil. This experience decided me to become a painter.

A painting by Monet always moves me, always teaches me something, and on my days of discouragement and doubt, a certain Monet has been a friend and guide to me.

And these Venice pictures, even better, in which everything unites as the expression of your will, in which no detail runs counter to emotion, in which you have achieved the sacrifice of genius that Delacroix recommended to us—I admire them as the highest incarnation of your art.

Signac to Monet
31 May 1912

The insulting criticisms of the early days left me cold, and I remain just as indifferent to the present praises of imbeciles, snobs, and wheeler-dealers. But the opinion of one or two people, among whom I include yourself, is precious to me.... I am sorry that your health has deprived me of the joy of talking with you.

Monet to Signac
Giverny, 5 June 1912

Monet and Denis

In the 1920s Monet was linked to the group of painters called the Nabis. In this New Year message he shows his interest in Maurice Denis' decorations for the Petit Palais.

This is to encourage you, and to offer you all my sympathy. I was very happy with the photograph of your work and can imagine what it must be like. Unfortunately, I have become thoroughly housebound and hardly ever come to Paris; but the day I do, I shall not fail to go to the Petit Palais.

Monet to Denis
Giverny, 4 January 1926

Monet and Kandinsky

Monet's Haystacks provided Wassily Kandinsky with a revelation that was to lead him to abstract art.

I experienced two events that set their seal on my entire life, and moved me in my deepest soul. These were the Impressionist Exhibition in Moscow

Wassily Kandinsky.

[winter, 1896–7], where I saw Monet's Haystacks, and a performance of Wagner.... Suddenly, for the first time, I *saw* a painting.... I dimly understood that the painting lacked an objective.... All of this was confusing to me, and I was incapable of drawing the most elementary conclusions from this experience. But one thing was quite clear: the undreamt-of power of the palette, which had hitherto been hidden from me. From it the painting received a force and a vividness that were fabulous. But also, unconsciously, the idea that an object is an indispensable element of any painting had been discredited.

Wassily Kandinsky
Rückblicke, 1913

Monet and Rodin

The friendship between the painter and the sculptor Auguste Rodin survived well beyond the Monet-Rodin Exhibition of 1889.

My dear Rodin,

I must tell you how overjoyed I am with the beautiful bronze you have sent me. I have put it in my studio so I shall be able to look at it all the time. I came back here filled with wonder at your *Gates* [*of Hell*] and at everything else I saw at your house.

Monet to Rodin
Giverny
25 May 1888

I have agreed to do an exhibition at Petit's gallery, of my paintings with Rodin's sculptures. It is a huge affair. The show will last three months during the Universal Exhibition, with an eye to the foreign public who will be visiting Paris then.

I therefore need a certain number of pictures, because I want a choice of what I have done in the past mingled with new things. So I am asking for your cooperation. This exhibition may have a certain success and will be a chance for you to make sales.

Monet to Paul Durand-Ruel
Fresselines
1 May 1889

Your letter delighted me, because you know that, bound up as we both are by our pursuit of nature, our friendships suffer. But the same constant feeling of brotherhood, the same love of art, has made us friends for all time, so I am happy to have your letter.

It must be very hard, at a certain age, to lose a friend or find him indifferent; at the very thought of it I also suffer, my dear friend. I have the same unchanging admiration for you as the painter who helped me understand the light, the clouds, the sea, and the cathedrals; I loved these things already, but their dawning beauty as revealed by you has touched me very deeply.

My best wishes to you then, my dear friend and companion, as well as to Mirbeau and Geffroy, whom I also love well.

Rodin to Monet
Montrozier (Aveyron)
22 September 1897

I got to the Salon only yesterday.... I have finally seen your *Balzac*. I was sure it would be beautiful, but it surpassed all my expectations; I tell you this in all sincerity.

You can forget the howls of the critics, you have never gone so far before; it is absolutely beautiful and great, it is superb, and I cannot stop thinking about it.

Monet to Rodin
Giverny, 30 June 1898

My dear friend,

You make me very happy with your appreciation of *Balzac*. Thank you. Your opinion is one of those which give me strength; I have had a torrent of abuse, not unlike what you had in the old days, when it was modish to laugh at your innovation of putting air into landscapes....

Your triumphant exhibition gives new strength to all artists who are persecuted as I am now. What an effect, one that has never been achieved before —and what a thing is that cathedral in the mist!

Your old friend.

Rodin to Monet
7 July 1898

You ask me to tell you what I think of Rodin. I wish to tell you of my deep admiration for this man, who is unique in our time, and a great man even among the very greatest.

Monet to the writer
Arsène Alexandre,
Giverny, 25 April 1900

My dear Maître,

My best wishes, Monet...and thank you for joining the committee for *The Thinker* and for your subscription.... Dear old friend, it is so good to be together again once in a while.

Your admirer.

Rodin to Monet
30 December 1904

My dear Rodin,

Thank you for your letter and your good wishes, which touched me very much. The next time I come to Paris, I will manage things so I can come and pay you a visit...and I also want to go and see how *The Thinker* looks at the Panthéon.

Your admirer and friend.

Monet to Rodin
Giverny, 2 January 1905

I wish to record my complete support for your project for a Musée Rodin; I

am happy to have this chance to show my admiration for this great artist.

Monet to Judith Cladel
Giverny, 20 December 1911

Monet and Maillol

In 1903, after Rodin, Aristide Maillol was foremost in Monet's appreciation of contemporary sculptors.

I deeply regret that Rodin has not been commissioned to do Zola's monument. To whom else can they apply? Well, to a young man with great promise who can give proof of it with just such a project. Maillol immediately springs to mind. He is the only one, apart from Rodin.

Monet to Duret
Giverny, 15 January 1903

Monet and Paul Nadar

This letter, addressed to the son of the celebrated photographer Nadar, who had lent his studio for the First Impressionist Exhibition in 1874, shows Monet's strong preference for "what is natural."

Dear Monsieur Nadar,

I hear you are to do a portrait of my stepson J.-P. Hoschedé and his fiancée and that you are inquiring about whether to use draperies. Personally, I would like you to photograph them as simply as possible, just as they are.

Note that I don't say as *well* as possible, since I know from experience that you get the best from your models. All I wish to do is remind you of my predilection for completely simple portraits, without props.

Thank you for the constancy of your friendship.

Monet to Paul Nadar
Giverny, 10 December 1903

Fervent and Discerning Critics

"One thing I am glad about is that I live in the same era as Monet." This remark, attributed to poet Stéphane Mallarmé, might have been made by any one of Monet's other writer friends. From the painter's first difficult beginnings, writers were important in his life; after his success (to which they contributed) they remained loyal to him in times of grief. "I need so badly to feel I have friends," Monet once wrote to Gustave Geffroy (26 December 1902).

Monet and Zola

Emile Zola noticed Monet's work the first time it appeared in the Salon; critic and painter soon became friends.

He has it in him to be a seascape painter of the highest order. But he understands the genre in his own way, and here again you note his deep love for immediate realities. In his seascapes there is always the end of a jetty, a corner of some quayside, something that indicates a date and a place. He seems to have a weakness for steamships. He loves the water like a mistress, he knows every piece in the hull of a vessel, he could put a name to the least line in her rigging.

I should probably admire these paintings very little, if Claude Monet were not a true painter. All I want to point out is the sympathy that draws him to modern subjects. But while I approve of his way of seeking out subject matter in the milieu he inhabits, I congratulate him even more for knowing how to paint, for having an exact, honest eye, for belonging to the great school of naturalists. What distinguishes his talent is his incredible ease of execution, his supple intelligence, his quick and lively understanding of any and every subject.

I have no fears for him. He will conquer the crowds whenever he chooses. Those who smile at the intentional harshness of his seascapes this year should remember his picture of his wife in a green dress in 1866. When a man can paint a fabric as beautifully as that, he knows his craft inside out, he has assimilated all the new methods,

Photograph of Emile Zola.

and he can do as he pleases. I expect nothing more from him save what is good, exact and true.

Emile Zola
"Mon Salon, IV, Les Actualistes"
L'Evénement Illustré, 24 May 1868

My dear Zola,

You have kindly sent me a copy of *L'Oeuvre*, and I thank you for it. I have always enjoyed reading your books, and this one is doubly interesting to me because it raises those questions about art for which we have been fighting so long. I have just read it, and I confess it has left me troubled and uneasy.

You have taken special care that not one of your characters should resemble one of us, but in spite of that I fear that our enemies in the press and the public will use the names of Manet and more or less all our friends as examples of failure, which I cannot believe is what you intend.

Excuse me for telling you this. It is not meant as a criticism. I have read *L'Oeuvre* with great pleasure, and every page raised some memory. Moreover you know I am a fanatical admirer of your talent. All the same I have been in the thick of it for a long time, and my experience leads me to worry that at the crucial moment our enemies will use your book to bludgeon us.

Monet to Zola
Giverny, 5 April 1886

My dear Zola,

Bravo once again and with all my heart, for your superb gallantry and courage [for writing his famous article, "J'accuse," *L'Aurore*, 13 January 1898]. Your old friend.

Monet to Zola
Giverny, 14 January 1898

Monet and Duret

The critic Théodore Duret, a connoisseur of Japanese art who had spent time in Japan, was one of the first buyers of Impressionist paintings. In 1878 he wrote a book on them, and in 1880 he supplied the preface to the catalogue of Monet's first private exhibition.

The first thought that came to mind in the presence of such complete series as Haystacks or Cathedrals was that Monet had somehow simplified his work by repeating the same subject over and over, and that he must have reached a point after the first two or three attempts where he could paint without difficulty. So it was thought that in executing his series he had set out to make his task easier and to produce the maximum of pictures with the minimum of effort. The truth is exactly the opposite. Since embarking on his series, he has actually produced fewer canvases than before. It turns out that painting different scenes, once only, was easier than producing many versions of the same scene in different guises. To catch on canvas, with precision, the various aspects of a scene, is an operation of great delicacy requiring exceptional vision. To paint like this one must grapple with real abstractions. One must contrive to separate the elusive theme from its unchanging background, and to do so in one fell swoop; for the different effects to be be grasped can, in their ephemerality, overlap one another, becoming confused if the eye does not arrest them of itself.

Monet bore up in his times of trial and sorrow with great force of character. Then, when success came to him, he was unaffected by it. He did not seek to obtain official advantages, as so many other artists are inclined to do, and in particular he refused to accept the Legion of Honor. He was ever a trusty friend to his Impressionist colleagues. He was the most able defender of Degas, Pissarro, Cézanne, Renoir, and Sisley; and he never ceased to express his deep admiration for Manet and to acknowledge everything he owed him.

He was perpetually intrigued by the spectacle of water. In the many different places where he worked, he introduced water as an integral part of his paintings. At Giverny, he painted the water he found there in many different ways. The water lilies and the reflections of his garden pool provided him with two of his most recent series; and now at the close of his career he returns to this subject in a singular manner. He approaches it as a decorative theme.

Théodore Duret
Histoire des Peintres Impressionistes
Paris, 1906, reprinted 1919

Monet and Maupassant

With their shared talent for "describing" landscape, Monet and Maupassant met several times at Etretat, notably in autumn 1885.

Several times last year I accompanied Claude Monet on his quest for impressions. At such times he was no longer a painter but a hunter. He went about followed by a gaggle of children who carried canvases, five or six at a time, representing the same subject at different times of day and with different effects.

He took the pictures up and

Guy de Maupassant.

abandoned them turn and turn about, according to the changing sky. And the painter, confronting his subject, waited and watched for the sun and the shadows, caught with a few brushstrokes a ray of sunshine or a cloud, and, scorning the false and the conventional, rapidly spread them on his canvas. I have seen him capture a glistening shaft of light on a white cliff, and fix it in a rush of yellow tones which made the effect of its elusive dazzlement strangely blinding and unsettling. Another time he appeared to seize a shower of rain on the sea in both hands and throw it against his canvas. And indeed it *was* the rain that he had painted in this way, nothing but rain veiling the waves, rocks and sky

which were barely discernible through
the downpour.

Guy de Maupassant,
"La Vie d'un Paysagiste,
(Etretat, Septembre),"
Gil Blas, 28 September 1886

Monet and Mallarmé

*Monet and Stéphane Mallarmé might
have left a collaborative work of art if
Monet had agreed to illustrate a text
by his friend. Declining, the painter
instead gave the writer a painting, on
13 July 1890, at Giverny. Berthe
Morisot was frequently the go-between
for the two men.*

My dear friend,
    Thank you for your kind letter. I am
very happy that you like my paintings
[*Antibes Seascapes,* which were exhibited
by Theo van Gogh at the Boussod-
Valadon Gallery], praise from such an
artist as yourself gives me great joy.

Monet to Mallarmé
19 June 1888

One may not disturb a man who is
rapt in the kind of joy that is given to
me by the contemplation of your
painting, dear Monet. I drown in its
brightness and consider that my
spiritual health stems from the fact
that I can always keep it more or less in
sight, according to the hours I keep.
I scarcely went to bed the first night,
for looking at it; and in the carriage
Mme. Manet [Berthe Morisot] was
ashamed that I only feared the lurchings
of the horse on my painting's
account.... You, sad? And you the only
being that no discouragement should
ever taint!

Mallarmé to Monet
Paris, 21 July 1890

*Monsieur Monet, que l'hiver ni
L'été sa vision ne leurre
Habite, en peignant, Giverny,
Sis auprès de Vernon dans l'Eure.*

[Monsieur Monet, who misses
    nothing
Either of winter, or of summer
Lives and paints at Giverny
Near Vernon, in the Eure.]

Mallarmé, on the envelope
of a letter to Monet,
Summer 1890

Monet and Proust

*Along with the paintings of Monet, Proust
mentions Giverny in his work. (Whether
he actually saw the house, or only
imagined it, is not certain.)*

What charming hours were those.
The sun shone full upon the loveliest
painting by Claude Monet that I know
of: *Tulip Fields Near Haarlem* [the
version of Tulip Fields bequeathed to
the Louvre by Winnaretta Singer,
Princess Edmond de Polignac; it is now
at the Musée d'Orsay, Paris]. Before his
marriage the prince had coveted this at
an auction, "but," he said, "to my fury
the thing was snatched from under my
nose by an American lady whose name
I immediately consigned to the fires of
hell. A few years later I married that
American lady and gained possession
of the painting!"
    Marcel Proust, under his pseudonym
"Horatio," in "Le Salon de la Princesse
Edmond de Polignac, Musique
d'Aujourdhui, Echos d'Autrefois,"
Le Figaro, 6 September 1903

Monet and Mirbeau

*Octave Mirbeau was one of the most
ardent defenders of Monet's art. Monet*

Octave Mirbeau.

read what he wrote and told Geffroy in 1890: "Mirbeau has become a master gardener. Gardening, and the Belgian Maeterlinck, are all he ever thinks about."

We had a very gay dinner; then we had to look at the paintings in the lamplight. First outpourings of enthusiasm from Mirbeau. We had to look at them again in the daylight, at which Mirbeau really went over the top; ... this evening the talk about art and literature kept me up after my usual bedtime.... Naturally I am happy when people like my pictures, but Mirbeau is really such a fanatic.

Monet to Alice Hoschedé
Belle-Ile, 4 November 1886

I went to spend a week with Monet on his island of Belle-Ile. And I await him on my island of Noirmoutier. He has done some very great paintings, revealing a new facet of his talent. Tremendous, formidable Monet....
He is a man of heroic courage, and if anyone deserves to succeed as well as you, it is he.

Mirbeau to Rodin
November 1886

Claude Monet understands that in order to achieve a more or less exact and emotive interpretation of nature, what should be painted in a landscape is not just its general lineaments, nor its partial details, nor the lie of its land and its greenery, but the moment you choose to paint it, when its character emerges; such is immediacy. Monet observed that on an average day, a given effect hardly lasts thirty minutes. Hence he had to tell the story of those thirty minutes, which is to say that in a given piece of nature, those minutes express both harmony in light, and harmony in concordant movements. This observation applies to figures, too (because these are really no more than a collection of shadows, lights, reflections and all things changing and shifting), just as it does to landscapes. The motif, and the instant of the motif, having been selected, Monet puts forth his first impression on the surface of the canvas.

Octave Mirbeau,
Preface for the catalogue of the
Monet-Rodin exhibition,
Georges Petit Gallery, Paris, 1889

Monet and Rolland

Romain Rolland was an avid frequenter of museums and galleries. Here he writes about Durand-Ruel's exhibition of Monet's Water Lilies in 1909.

CE QUE L'ON A VU AU SALON DE L'AUTOMOBILE

Scene from Sacha Guitry's 1918 play *Histoire de France* in which Monet (played by Guitry himself) and Clemenceau (Jean Péricr) meet at Giverny.

I admire you most of all, among today's French artists.

Art such as yours is the glory of a nation and of an era. When I am a little digusted by the mediocrity of modern music and literature, I need only turn to painting, where works like your Water Lilies are blossoming, to reconcile myself with the art of our time, and to believe that it stands comparison with the greatest that has gone before. I have admired your work for over twenty years, from the time when I was still at [school] and saw an exhibition of yours (the Belle-Ile paintings of rocks beaten by the sea).

Rolland to Monet
14 June 1909

Monet and Guitry

The playwright Sacha Guitry, who was a frequent visitor to Giverny and often received Monet at his house at Yainville, sent the painter tickets to the dress rehearsals and first nights of his plays.

I have just received two tickets for Sacha's dress rehearsal [*Faisons un Rêve*, at the Bouffes-Parisiens Theatre, 3 October 1916]. I am coming up tomorrow with my stepdaughter, and we hope to see you at the theater.

Monet to G. or J. Bernheim-Jeune
Giverny, 2 October 1916

My dear Sacha,
I am most touched by your letter and your good wishes. I shall never forget those happy times at your house with our dear friend Mirbeau.

Monet to Guitry
Giverny, 5 January 1923

Monet and Geffroy

Monet first met Gustave Geffroy at Belle-Ile in 1886. After more than thirty years spent analyzing his friend's artistic development, the art critic published a book about him.

Well, my dear Geffroy, you were supposed to let me know when you were coming here, and already a month has passed. Come on, bestir yourself a little and name a day, any day, as long as it is soon.... I have received your article on my exhibition. Many thanks. You are always the one who says best whatever there is to say, and it is always a pleasure for me to be praised by you. ... Your old friend.

Monet to Geffroy
Giverny, 1 June 1909

In fact, his work resembles nothing else in the history of art. If he had continued with his figurative studies, he could have produced an evocation of the modern world, of people and of theater. But he left all that to pursue an ever more complex, magical, and evocative form of representation, of aspects of nature as revealed by light. His work is a revelation and a poem, which unveils a universe that nobody before him has ever perceived.

Gustave Geffroy
Claude Monet, Sa Vie, Son Oeuvre
1922 (Introduction)

My dear friend,

I had just written you a letter when your book arrived, with its kind dedication. I need not tell you how touched I am, all modesty apart, by the good things you say about my work and myself.... For all that you have written so well of my life and labors (I have naturally left aside everything which is documentation, despite the interest it may have for others), I thank you from the bottom of my heart... thank you again for all the beautiful things in this book.

Your old friend.

Monet to Geffroy
Giverny, 25 June 1922

Monet and Clemenceau

The politician-turned-art-critic, who had once been a doctor, spent many hours comforting Monet over his cataract problems. Monet appreciated Clemenceau's affection during his last years.

Dear friend,

I thought I had discerned that the man in you was worthy of the artist.... But now, without my permission, you bombard me with this monstrous lump of light [*The Bloc,* a painting done on the Creuse, which Monet presented to Clemenceau]. I am still groggy and I don't know what more to say. You cut out chunks of the sky and hurl them at people's heads. Nothing would be more idiotic than to thank you for this. One cannot thank a sunbeam.

I salute you with all my heart.

Clemenceau to Monet
Paris, 23 December 1899

My dear Clemenceau,

I sent you a telegram this morning to express my joy, but I still want you to know how grateful I am for what you have just done for Manet. [Because of Clemenceau's intervention, the *Olympia* had just been transferred from the Musée du Luxembourg to the Louvre.]

I understood the other day that you would do what I had asked of you, and I thank you with all my heart.

Monet to Clemenceau
Giverny, 8 February 1907

And now my old friend Clemenceau is in power. What a burden; may he do good work despite all the traps that will be set for him! What magnificent energy he has, nonetheless!

Monet to G. or J. Bernheim-Jeune
Giverny, 26 November 1917

My dear and great friend,

I am on the brink of completing two decorative panels, and would ask you if you will offer them to the State. It is a small gesture, but the only way I have of participating in France's victory.

I admire and salute you with all my heart.

Monet to Clemenceau
12 November 1918

Clemenceau is faithful as ever, and comes often to see me. It seems to do him good to come and talk things over, and he cheers me up, too. What a man!

Monet to Geffroy
Giverny, 8 December 1919

Monet and England

M. Monet's constant study of natural effects has produced in his mind a complete divergence from those ideas about landscape colour which are born and bred in studios in great cities. The city painter fancies that nature is grey or brown, with a little dull green on grass, or permissible pale blue in the sky towards the top of the picture. M. Monet has seen the real colouring of nature—seas of sapphire and emerald, or dark purple and violet far away, cliffs of brilliant white or stained with reds incredible to the citizen critic, and confused medleys of the richest colours in weedy pools upon the sands. He has seen the Atlantic waves beat wildly on the purple rocks of Brittany; he has studied the Mediterranean, with its pale, pure blues and greens, dark by comparison with the sun-baked fortifications of Antibes and the aërial radiance of the distant maritime Alps. For variety of observation, joined to complete singleness of purpose in each separate work, no French landscape-painter is comparable to Claude Monet. The utmost dreariness of a frozen river and a snowed-up little town in Normandy, the summer glory of the south, the burning autumnal foliage by some quiet trout-stream in contrast with the persistent green of its grassy bank, are all equally interesting to this open-minded observer; and each separate phase of nature that he represents occupies him exclusively at the time, so that there is never any confusion in his mind between one motive and another. Yet for many years Monet has been a most unpopular artist, and his unpopularity has been due both to his merits and his defects. First, he sees and imitates natural colour...colour that always puzzles and amazes the unobservant; and he tries to raise the key of his tonality as high as he can towards the exalted pitch of natural light—two endeavours that are sure to make pictures look glaring, especially whilst the paint is fresh. In colour and light Claude Monet does not paint what other people expect or want to see, but tries for what he has himself seen in nature. Next, he has the purest possible landscape instinct, not seeking much or often for adventitious human interest...as prudent moderns have done generally. A lonely place is interesting for him if it has natural beauty or character—or even an effect may make it interesting. Now, as to imperfections, although M. Monet is said by his friends to be a good draughtsman when he chooses, he puts very little drawing into his painting; he is not half so sensitive to the beauty of form which exists in natural landscape as he is to its glory of colour and brilliance of light, and for those who love the delicate beauty of form, this inattention to it is vexatious. The desire for broad truth of colour and effect has caused M. Monet to pass over natural detail, which has an infinite charm for many who love nature as sincerely as he does himself, but in a different way.

Philip Hamerton,
"The Present State of the Fine Arts in France: Impressionism,"
Portfolio, February 1891

Monet at His Easel

Monet was always an enemy of theories; one of his favorite comments was that "a painter has better things to do than write." He rarely revealed his ideas about art. Nevertheless, his letters yield interesting bits of information on his way of working and his approach to subject matter. They show how important painting was to him, and how it was even (in his own words) an obsession.

Drawing—"With the Brush and With Color"

Here Monet defines himself as a painter.

Dear Sir,
    I have no idea how to answer you... since I only draw with the brush and with color, and have always refused (even when asked by my closest friends) to attempt a style of work about which I know nothing. I am very sorry to have to refuse your request.... I do still possess one or two rare sketches I did in my youth, but they are neither very interesting nor worthy of being reproduced.
    Monet to an unknown correspondent
Giverny, 5 April 1914

Painting in the Presence of Nature

I had two studies, of apple trees loaded with fruit, which I had to abandon. When I arrived at the place where I was to work, there were *no more apples—* they had all been picked. Which means two more canvases wasted...this is discouraging.
    How I envy people who can paint from memory.

Monet to Duret
Vétheuil, 3 October 1880

No, I am not a great painter, nor a great poet.... I only know that I do what I can to express what I feel in the presence of nature.

Monet to Geffroy
Giverny, 7 June 1912

I have always had a horror of theories... my only merit is that I have painted directly from nature, seeking to convey my impressions of her most elusive effects: and I am aghast at being the cause of a name given to a group of artists of whom the majority were anything but Impressionists.

Monet to Evan Charteris
Giverny
21 June 1926

"The Sea, Which Is Very Much My Element"

Monet made this claim during his stay in Bordighera, which began on 3 March 1884. Throughout his life Monet went out of his way to paint the sea.

You know my passion for the sea, and this particular one is so beautiful. Trained as I am, and constantly observing it, I am sure I would manage to do some excellent things if I could live here for a few more months. I feel I understand the sea better every day, the bitch, and it is certain that the way she is here that name is appropriate, for she is very terrible; she has one of those tones of dull blue-green....

In short, I adore the sea, but I know that to do her justice you have to view her every day, at all hours, and from the same point of vantage, so as to learn how she lives.

Monet to Alice Hoschedé
Belle-Ile
30 October 1886

And now come his first seascapes: the Channel, Le Havre, Trouville, Honfleur, the sea caught in its most mysterious rhythms, captured in its mistiest distance, with solitudes lulled by the perpetual lamentation of waves; its swarms of boats, its sandy beaches, cliffs, and rocks; the sea, one of the great passions of Monet's life, through which, magnificent poet that he is, he conveys in physical terms his heart-rending awareness of the infinite.

Octave Mirbeau,
Preface to the catalogue for the
Monet-Rodin exhibition, 1889

On the "Series" Paintings

From the first, the method for Monet's series (Haystacks, Poplars, and Cathedrals) was systematized to its logical limit; the canvases were completed in his studio, and often with a view to their effect as a group. As a result Monet was accused of working from photographs.

No, I am not in London save in my thoughts, since I am working exclusively at painting.... For the work I am doing, I need to have them all in view, and to tell you the truth, not one has actually been completed. I inch them forward all together, or at least several at a time.

Monet to Durand-Ruel
Giverny, 23 March 1903

Harrison said all kinds of spiteful things and criticized everything. He said, "Monet is covering a mass of canvases in his studio; just recently he asked me to send him photographs of the bridges in London and of Parliament so he could finish his views of the Thames."

Durand-Ruel to Monet
Paris, 11 February 1905

Dear Monsieur Durand,

You are quite wrong to worry about the things you tell me, which attest to nothing more than ill will and jealousy and which leave me absolutely cold. I know Mr. Harrison. Sargent asked him to take a small photo of Parliament for me, which I was never able to use. But that means very little, and whether my Cathedrals, my Londons, and my other pictures are done from life or not is my affair and anyway is of no importance whatever. I know plenty of painters who work from life and produce nothing but hideous things.

Monet to Durand-Ruel
Giverny, 12 February 1905

Like you, I am sorry not to be able to exhibit the Water Lily series this year.... It is not because I want to show a lot of them at once that I am delaying the exhibition—absolutely not—but because I really have too few satisfactory ones to justify alarming the public.... Moreover, it would be very bad to show the few I have in the series so far, since the desired effect can only be produced by displaying them all together. In addition to this, I need to have the completed things here where I can see them, so I can compare them with the ones I plan to do.

Monet to Durand-Ruel
Giverny, 27 April 1907

"My Work Belongs to the Public"

Monet's pictures are the best guide to the artist. Monet himself was always very reticent: "I confine myself to my brushes," he wrote succinctly to Louis Vauxcelles (28 September 1900).

I am old and I live a retired life. I loathe self-advertisement, interviews, and the like. People can talk about and discuss my work, but my life is nobody's business but mine.

Monet to André Arnyvelde
Giverny, 19 November 1913

I was hoping you would completely give up your idea, and that made me happy since I hardly like being made

M onet often received friends and visitors in his studio (c. 1900).

conspicuous, and (without any false modesty) do not believe I deserve it at all. As a painter I have done what I could, and that is quite enough for me. I don't like to be compared to the great masters of the past, and it is quite sufficient that my painting is open to critical appraisal. You know my fondness for M. Fénéon. I will be delighted to receive him and talk with him, but I draw the line at dictating my memoirs.

Monet to G. or J. Bernheim-Jeune
Giverny, 24 November 1918

My works belong to the public, and the public can say what it likes about them. I have done my best; but I refuse to be bothered with questions, and see no reason why I should.

Monet to Geffroy
Giverny, 20 January 1920

"Painting Is Such Torture!"

I am fairly happy with the results of my stay here, even though the studies I have done are far from what I had hoped. It is appallingly difficult. I think there's hardly anybody left like me, hardly anyone who won't stand for half measures. Well, my friend, I will struggle and scrape and start anew, and it seems to me when I look out at nature that I am going to do everything, record everything, and to hell with all else when work's in progress....

All this goes to show one must think of painting and of nothing else. Only by observation and thought can one find the way.

Monet to Bazille
Honfleur, 15 July 1864

For a month I've been unable to do anything decent. I've scraped off and torn up just about all my work. I am very disgusted with myself; a superb summer wasted. Painting is such torture! And I am no good at all.

Monet to Caillebotte
Giverny, 4 September 1887

When you ask Monet about his art, you know straightaway that he has never been happy with his work, as compared to his dream of what it could be. He has glimpsed the limitless poetry of light and atmosphere, and he believes himself incapable of capturing it. He is quite wrong.

Gustave Geffroy
Claude Monet, Sa Vie, Son Oeuvre
1922 (Preface)

"All My Time Is Given to Painting"

Working at his easel in the garden at Giverny, Monet tried to forget his personal grief, war, and the cataracts that were increasingly affecting his sight.

I am back at work. It's still the best way to avoid thinking too much of the current miseries, although I am a little ashamed to be thinking of infinitesimal researches in form and color when so many people are suffering and dying for our sakes.

Monet to Geffroy
Giverny, 1 December 1914

I am a slave to my work, forever in pursuit of the impossible.... I have little time left to live and I must give all of it to painting, in the hope that I will finally achieve something fine, which if it is possible will also satisfy me.

Monet to G. Bernheim-Jeune
Giverny, 3 August 1918

I am caught up in my work with no thought for anything else, so happy am I to see colors again. It is truly a resurrection.

Monet to G. Bernheim-Jeune
Giverny, 6 October 1925

My dear good friend,

I was so much better that I thought of getting my brushes and palette ready for work again, but relapses and new pain kept me from doing so. I am still in high hopes and am busy with major alterations to my studio and changes for the better in the garden. All this to show you that my courage is high and I am in control.... Also, if I do not gain the strength to do my panels as I would like to, I have decided to give them as they are, or at least some of them.

Yours more than ever.

Monet to Clemenceau
Giverny, 18 September 1926

The "Painter's Garden" at Giverny

From the beginning, and throughout his years at Argenteuil and Vétheuil, Monet was interested in gardens and represented them in his paintings. When he moved to Giverny in 1883, he became an "artist-gardener," indulging his passion for flowers and creating an extraordinary water garden.

Clemenceau, Monet, and Lily Butler on the Japanese bridge, 1921.

"And Are There Still Flowers in the Garden?"

Monet's thoughts were seldom far from Giverny. He questioned Alice constantly about the state of the garden, worried about the effect of weather on his flowers, and gave instructions for the greenhouse.

And are there still flowers in the garden? I hope there will still be chrysanthe-mums when I get home. If it freezes, make beautiful bouquets of them.

Monet to Alice Hoschedé
Etretat, 24 November 1885

Thank you for taking care of my beloved flowers; you are a good gardener. There's no pressing need to lift the gladioli, but when you do I

The Monet-Hoschedé family gathered at Giverny. Monet stands at left, behind Alice.

recommend hardy perennials, like anemones and my pretty clematis.

Monet to Alice Hoschedé
Belle-Ile, 2 November 1886

I have found some wallflowers at last. Several baskets of them are on their way to Vernon. There are some very good gardeners here.... In one of the baskets will be other plants, some perennials, passiflora for the greenhouse, some very pretty yellow flowers, and two curious little nasturtiums.

Monet to Alice Monet
Rouen, 7 March 1893

What you say about my poor little roses is very worrying, and I fear plenty of other disasters. Did anyone think at least to cover the Japanese peonies? It would have been plain murder not to do so. I'm dying to see the greenhouse, and I hope it will still be beautiful. What bliss it will be to come home again!

Monet to Alice Monet
Sandviken, 17 March 1895

"I Hate to Leave Giverny, Especially Now That I Am Arranging the House and Garden as I Want Them"

Monet made this remark to Mallarmé a few months after buying his new property.

I remain as domestic as ever, delighting in the lovely things around me.

Monet to Geffroy
Giverny, 23 August 1900

Dear friends,
I would be a liar if I told you I am not happy to be back with my family, and to see my flowers again.

Monet to Sacha Guitry
and Charlotte Lysès,
Giverny, 25 August 1913

Thank you for your offer to remove my pictures, but in spite of what people are saying, and although the Musée de Rouen has been evacuated, I refuse to believe I shall ever be forced to leave Giverny. As I have already written, I prefer to die here surrounded by everything I have made.

Monet to G. Bernheim-Jeune
Giverny, 21 June 1918

What is happening to me, you have readily guessed. I am working, and not without difficulty, because my sight is going a little more each day. I am also very busy in my garden, which is a joy to me, and in this lovely weather we have been having I am exultant, reveling in nature. With all this, there is no time to be bored.

Monet to G. Bernheim-Jeune
Giverny, 23 February 1920

Gardening and Flowers: A Passion Shared With Other Initiates

Monet's old friends were always being invited to admire his garden. Mallarmé sent him affectionate poems, other friends exchanged their paintings with him, and still others exchanged flowers.

The countryside is so lovely, I wanted to write and ask you to come and see the garden, which is beautiful at present: worth the trip, and in fifteen or so days it will be over.

Monet to Geffroy
Giverny, 25 May 1900

I am still awaiting your promised visit. This is the moment you will see a splendid garden. But you must hurry.... Any later and there will be no flowers. Work it out with Geffroy and write to me. I am counting on you. Also I have a pile of new pictures. With my best wishes. Bully Geffroy a bit and come down.

Monet to Clemenceau
Giverny, 29 May 1900

I will arrange to have the roses I ordered sent as quickly as possible, and will go to Yainville with the plants I plan to give you…and put the whole lot down in front of me.

Monet to Charlotte Lysès
and Sacha Guitry,
Giverny, 31 March 1914

I have sent to you, care of the Sables railway station, a basket of aubretias, the violet border you like. I think they should come on well in your soil, if planted in the sun.... I also want to send you some Pennsylvania roses, which grow very well by the sea.

Monet to Clemenceau
Giverny, 29 September 1923

I would be very happy to see you. I will let Monet know, and we can have a charming day together. We'll talk paintings and flowers and boats, three things we all adore!

Mirbeau to Caillebotte
(undated)

"An Interior...to Our Taste"

The house at Giverny thus described by Monet (to Alice, from Norway, 31 January 1895) was inseparable from the garden. Supported by Alice, an accomplished housekeeper, Monet shared his way of life with his guests. An interest in cooking and delicious food served, among other things, to unite his circle of friends.

My dear Mallarmé,
    Would you be kind enough to send me your recipe for chanterelles? There are lots about at the moment, and in my greediness I remembered your promise.

Monet to Mallarmé
Giverny, 21 July 1890

This house, though modest, is nonetheless sumptuous on account of its interior and the garden, or rather, the gardens that surround it. The man who has conceived and established this small, familiar, magnificent world of his own is not only a great artist in the creation of his paintings, but also in the environment he has made for himself, for his own delight. This house and garden are likewise a work of art, and

Menu for the wedding luncheon of Germaine Hoschedé at Giverny, 12 November 1902.

Monet has invested his life in the creating and perfecting of it.

Gustave Geffroy
Claude Monet, Sa Vie, Son Oeuvre
1922

Japan in a Normandy Garden

The orchard, or clos normand, *which lay beneath the windows of the house at Giverny, gradually yielded to the garden created by Monet, filled with flowers and flowering shrubs from Japan. Monet's borrowings from Japanese gardens are even more evident in his*

water garden, with its bridge, bamboos, and water lilies.

Thank you for thinking of me for the Hokusai flowers [Japanese prints]…. You say nothing of the poppies, and that is what is most important, for I already have the irises, the chrysanthemums, the peonies, and the volubilis.
> Monet to Maurice Joyant
> Giverny, 8 February 1896

Here we have masses of flowers; the plums, Japanese apricots, and narcissi are blossoming…our weeping willows are completely green.
> Monet to Jean-Pierre Hoschedé
> Giverny, 8 February 1916

I was flattered by your two letters, having the deepest admiration for Japanese art and great sympathy for the Japanese…. I received your lovely prints with profound pleasure.
> Monet to Shintaro Yamashita
> Giverny, 19 February 1920

"A Place of Tints and Hues, More Than of Blossoms"

The world Monet created was an inspiration for many writers, who grasped the originality of the "painter's garden."

Personally, one may say that the Giverny work is the most triumphant exposition of the methods of Impressionism. If the series known as "Les Cathédrales" be added, one may safely challenge the most critical. It is natural that Giverny should inspire the finest harvest, for, after years of experimental residence, it is here that Monet finally settled in 1883. The dominant note in the Giverny paintings is one of joy in the beauty of life and

Monet and Geffroy in front of the Japanese bridge, photographed by Sacha Guitry in around 1920.

nature. They are the works of an inspired genius, who never forgets that Beauty is the mission of Art.

Monet is seen in his most genial moods when, with cigar for company, he strolls through his "propriété" at Giverny, discussing the grafting of plants and other agricultural mysteries with his numerous blue-bloused and sabotted gardeners….

After painting, Monet's chief recreation is gardening. In his domain at Giverny, and in his Japanese water-garden across the road and railway (which to his lasting sorrow cuts his little world in twain), each season of the year brings its appointed and distinguishing colour scheme. Nowhere else can be found such a prodigal display of rare and marvellously beautiful colour effects, arranged from flowering plants gathered together without regard to expense from every quarter of the globe.

In the neighbouring fields are hundreds of poplars standing in long lines. These trees, which inspired "Les Peupliers," were bought by Monet to avoid the wholesale destruction which threatened every tree in the Seine valley a few years ago. The building authorities of the Paris Exhibition required materials for palisading, and thousands of trees were ruthlessly felled to make a cosmopolitan holiday.

In the peace of Giverny we leave the great painter. He is one of the few original members of the Impressionist group who has lived to see the almost complete reversal of the hostile judgment passed upon his canvases by an ill-educated public. Now he is able to enjoy not only the satisfaction of having his principles acknowledged, but also the receipt of the material fruits of a world-wide renown. Not often do pioneers succeed so thoroughly.

Wynford Dewhurst
Impressionist Painting, 1904

Giverny Reborn—in 1980

Monet's property was bequeathed by his second son, Michel, to the Académie des Beaux-Arts. Extensive restoration has since been carried out on the house and garden.

It is essential to make the pilgrimage to the flowered sanctuary of Giverny, the better to understand the master, to grasp the sources of his inspiration, and to imagine him still living among us.

Gérald van der Kemp
Preface to Claire Joyes
Claude Monet: Life at Giverny, 1985

The Orangerie: Monet's Testament

Monet died in 1926, before he knew the fate of the Grandes Décorations *he had offered to the French State. Reservations were expressed by some, who saw in the work the end of Impressionism. But most of the artists and thinkers of the century felt deep admiration for it; some have even detected a cosmic, sacred dimension in the "chapel" of the Orangerie, which was conceived according to the painter's wishes and unveiled on 17 May 1927.*

8 July 1927. At the Orangerie, in two large, oval rooms, the Water Lilies of Claude Monet. Mirrors of water in which the water lilies flower at all hours of the day, morning, afternoon, evening, and night. Claude Monet, at the end of his long life, after studying everything that the different motifs afforded by nature could give him in answer to the question of light's relation to ensembles of colour, concluded by addressing himself to the element that is in itself the most docile and penetrable —water, the epitome of transparency, iridescence, and reflection. Thanks to water, he has made himself the indirect painter of what we do not see. He concentrates on the almost invisible, spiritual surface that divides light from

its own reflection. The blue of the sky imprisoned in liquid blue. The only evidence of a surface is the flowers, their whorls of leaves and petals, vegetable emanations of the deep, bubbles, opening eggs. The canvases are glued to the wall in long concave bands that envelop the spectator, who views them both frontally and laterally. The light is beaten into blue, through the chemistry of water. Claude Monet feels the same passion for color as those who made the stained glass for our cathedrals. Color rises from the depths of the water in clouds and whirlpools.

Paul Claudel
Journal, 1904–32
8 July 1927

So much has Monet been attracted by the analysis of the laws of light that he has made light the real subject of all his pictures, and to show clearly his intention he has treated one and the same site in a series of pictures painted from nature at all hours of the day. This is the principle whose results are the great divisions of his work, which might be called "Investigation of the variations of sunlight." The most famous of these series are the "Haystacks," the "Poplars," the "Cliffs of Etretat," the "Golfe Juan," the "Cathedrals," the "Water Lilies," and finally the "Thames" series upon which Monet is at present engaged. They are like great poems, and the splendor of the chosen theme, the orchestration of the shivers of brightness, the symphonic *parti-pris* of the colors, make their realism, the minute contemplation of reality, approach idealism and lyric dreaming....

His recent series of Water Lilies expressed all the melancholic and fresh charm of quiet pools, of sweet stretches of water blocked by rushes and calyxes. He has painted underwoods in the autumn, where the most subtle shades of bronze and gold are at play, chrysanthemums, pheasants, roofs at twilight, dazzling sunflowers, gardens, tulip-fields in Holland, bouquets....

Monet excels also in suggesting the *drawing of light*, if I may venture to use this expression. He makes us understand the movement of the vibrations of heat, the movement of the luminous waves; he also understands how to paint the sensation of strong wind. "Before one of Monet's pictures," said Mme. Morisot, "I always know which way to incline my umbrella." Monet is also an incomparable painter of water. Pond, river, or sea—he knows how to differentiate their coloring, their consistency, and their currents, and he transfixes a moment of their fleeting life. He is intuitive to an exceptional degree in the intimate composition of matter, water, earth, stone or air, and this intuition serves him in place of intellectuality in his art. He is a painter par excellence, a man born for painting, and this power of penetrating the secrets of matter and of light helps him to attain a kind of grand, unconsciously lyrical poetry. He transposes the immediate truth of our vision and elevates it to decorative grandeur. If Manet is the realist-romanticist of Impressionism, if Degas is its psychologist, Claude Monet is its lyrical pantheist.

His work is immense. He produces with astonishing rapidity, and he has yet another characteristic of the great painters: that of having put his hand to every kind of subject. His recent studies of the Thames are, at the decline of his

Georges Clemenceau around 1900 (left); plan of the Orangerie (below); Monet's Water Lilies in the Orangerie, c. 1930 (right).

Dissenting Views

A seascape that could be turned upside down, for example, would be a bad painting. Turner himself, otherwise so daring in his luminous phantasms, never risked painting a *reversible* seascape, one in which the sky could be

energetic maturity, as beautiful and as spontaneous as the Haystacks of seventeen years back. They are thrillingly truthful visions of fairy mists, where showers of silver and gold sparkle through rosy vapors; and at the same time Monet combines in this series the dream-landscapes of Turner with Monticelli's accumulation of precious stones. Thus interpreted by this intense faculty of synthesis, nature, simplified in detail and contemplated in its grand lines, becomes truly a living dream.

Camille Mauclair
The French Impressionists 1860–1900
1903

taken for water and the water for sky. And if Monet the Impressionist has done this in his equivocal Water Lily series, one can say that he has sought his penitence in sin; for never have Monet's Water Lilies been, nor will they ever be, held as a serious event in the history of art. Rather they will be viewed as a caprice which, though it pleases for a moment, fails otherwise in every way to gain admittance to the nobler archives of our memory. They are a brief diversion; they are intimately related with a purely decorative element, like the products of industrial art; they are akin to arabesques, tapestries, Faenza plates; they are something, finally, that one sees without looking, grasps without thought, and forgets without remorse.

Eugenio d'Ors
La Vie de Goya, 1928

The work in which Monet freed himself from all vestige of tradition, but lost his first freshness, is shown very lavishly in two special rooms containing panels intended by the master "for eternity," which represent water lilies on the pond of his property at Giverny. The result exudes a kind of misdirected superiority; and certainly admirers of

Monet who have tolerated this have not served Monet's memory well.

No doubt there are certain qualities in the Water Lilies. Not everybody can do such things; if one examines these "smeared expanses" with love, one sees in them the technical experimentation and sonority of Monet's palette. Nevertheless, what emptiness, what an obvious lack of understanding, what a strange and truly pitiful crowning is this, to the career of the painter of *Woman in Green* and *The Picnic*! What a shame that the demands of creative research should at such a moment have obliged the artist to betray his early investigations; what vanity can have enticed him into this realm of monumental decoration, when he was really not at all gifted in the field? And finally, how ironic that France, which in earlier days had airily permitted the snatching away of her glorious son's most wonderful masterpieces, should at last erect for his feeblest and most overrated work an entire temple, which more than anything else resembles the saloon deck of a transatlantic liner!

Alexandre Benois
on the Monet Exhibition
at the Orangerie, 1931,
from *Alexandre Benois Refléchit*, 1968

The Water Lilies at the Orangerie are a fully constructed work of art, and the real lily pool is present not as model, but as master.... One may see to what degree the late work of Monet is absolutely a thing of the mind.

There are broad fringes of reeds and bankside rushes; woolly, vertical treetrunks in the second room; narrow vertical fringes of willow foliage; roughened surfaces of clouds that are the wrong way up, horizontal and more or less elongated, and rippling on the skin of the water; broad enveloping flourishes for water lily leaves with blazing flecks for flowers. In short, we are faced with a complete system of coded signals.

The raising of the horizon, which was formerly such a feature of Monet's work, is now complete, for the sky and the distance no longer appear, save in their inverted form, and the water surface rises vertically all around us, as in a dream of flying or diving....

In the real-life pool at Giverny, the water would have turned the world topsy-turvy even had there been no flowers; but in Monet's work of art the flowers are the only figurative element.

Michel Butor
Art de France, 1963

Monet dedicated his final years to his lyrical series of Water Lilies. I was surprised to find myself taking off my hat to the man. When a reality provokes so decisive a reaction, there can be no denying it: The work is strong and noble. Despite his apparent superficiality, Monet, like Matisse, achieves results of as great consequence as certain much more severe works. The chapel-like presentation and the aquarium light contribute to this

powerful impression, but all the same, Monet himself has a great deal to do with it.

Amédée Ozenfant
entry for 27 June 1931
Mémoires 1886–1962, 1968

We may dream of Claude Monet moving toward the use of broad, clear expanses like Veronese or Tiepolo. Let us dream no more, and consider his supreme work, the Water Lilies. Despite their monumental dimensions, the Water Lilies show none of the characteristics of great Flemish and Venetian decorative art. Monet's mental disposition here seems to me to have been that of a great easel painter, who has decided to endow his vision with a field broad enough to encompass the whole world. Here a mirror of water suffices for our identification with the universe. A cosmic vision, I would prefer to say, if that word had not been hijacked recently, and used to describe just about anyone and anything. Thus Michelangelo, a creator of solitary, unique figures, had to await the day when the Vatican would allow him to take wing, to show his power. For this reason it gives me profound delight to say of the Orangerie that it is truly the Sistine Chapel of Impressionism. A deserted place in the heart of Paris, it lends an element of sacred inaccessibility to the masterpiece it contains; which is one of the supreme achievements of French genius.

André Masson,
"Monet, le Fondateur,"
Verve, vol. VII, nos. 27
and 28, 1952

Further Reading

CATALOGUE OF THE ARTIST'S WORK

Wildenstein, Daniel, et al., *Claude Monet, Biographie et Catalogue Raisonné*, 4 vols., 1974–85; 5th volume in preparation. This important work, on which this book is largely based, includes Monet's published correspondence.

GENERAL TITLES

Gordon, Robert, and Andrew Forge, *Claude Monet*, Harry N. Abrams, New York, 1984

Herbert, Robert L., *Impressionism: Art, Leisure and Parisian Society*, Yale University Press, New Haven, Connecticut, 1988

House, John, *Impressionist Masterpieces: National Gallery of Art, Washington, D.C.*, Outlet Book Co., Avenal, New Jersey, 1989

——, *Monet: Nature into Art*, Yale University Press, New Haven, Connecticut, 1988

Joyes, Claire, *Claude Monet: Life at Giverny*, Vendome Press, New York, 1985

Kendall, Richard (ed.), *Monet by Himself*, Bulfinch Press, New York, 1990

Rewald, John, *The History of Impressionism*, 4th revised edition, Museum of Modern Art, New York, 1973

Seitz, William C., *Monet*, Harry N. Abrams, New York, 1984

Spate, Virginia, *The Colour of Time: Claude Monet*, Thames and Hudson, London, 1992

Tucker, Paul Hayes, *Monet at Argenteuil*, Yale University Press, New Haven, Connecticut, 1982

——, *Monet in the Nineties: The Series Paintings* (Stephen R. Frankel, ed.), Museum of Fine Arts, Boston, 1989

Wildenstein, Daniel, *Monet's Years at Giverny: Beyond Impressionism*, Harry N. Abrams, New York, 1978

EXHIBITION CATALOGUES

Hommage à Monet, Grand Palais, Paris, 1980

Monet in Holland, Rijksmuseum Vincent van Gogh, Amsterdam, 1986

Monet in London, High Museum of Art, Atlanta, Georgia, 1988–9

Monet in the Nineties: The Series Paintings, Museum of Fine Arts, Boston; Art Institute of Chicago; Royal Academy of Arts, London, 1990

Monet-Rodin, Centenaire de l'Exposition de 1889, Musée Rodin, Paris, 1989–90

Monet's Years at Giverny: Beyond Impressionism, Metropolitan Museum of Art, New York, 1978

Museums

Nearly two thousand paintings by Monet have been identified. Many may be viewed in museums around the world.

UNITED STATES

There are fine examples of Monet's work in museums throughout the United States, including the Museum of Fine Arts, Boston; the Art Institute of Chicago; the Los Angeles County Museum of Art; the Museum of Modern Art and the Metropolitan Museum of Art, New York; the Philadelphia Museum of Art; and the National Gallery of Art, Washington, D.C.

FRANCE

In France there are about thirty paintings by the artist in provincial museums. In Paris three museums are very rich in his paintings: The Musée Marmottan has a collection derived from the Donop de Monchy Bequest and the bequest of Michel Monet, the painter's second son; the Musée d'Orsay possesses about sixty paintings by Monet; and the Orangerie in the Tuileries Gardens includes two rooms dedicated to the Water Lilies. Also, the Petit Palais and the Musée Rodin each contain a few works by Monet. Finally, the Musée Claude Monet at Giverny, though it contains no original work by the painter, has been open to the public since 1980.

The gardens, greenhouses, water lily pool, house, and studios are all of particular interest to visitors, being closely linked to Monet's work in his last years.

GREAT BRITAIN

Collections include those of the Fitzwilliam Museum, Cambridge; the National Museum of Wales, Cardiff; the Courtauld Institute Galleries, London; and the National Gallery, London.

List of Illustrations

All works are by Claude Monet unless otherwise indicated.

Abbreviations: *a*=above; *b*=below; *c*=center; *l*=left; *r*=right; BN=Bibliothèque Nationale, Paris

Front cover *The Garden at Giverny* (detail). Oil on canvas, 81 x 92 cm, 1900. Musée d'Orsay, Paris
Spine *Turkeys* (detail). Oil on canvas, 174.5 x 172.5 cm, 1876–7. Musée d'Orsay, Paris
Back cover *Impression, Sunrise.* Oil on canvas, 48 x 63 cm, 1872–3. Formerly Musée Marmottan, Paris
1a*l The Garden at Giverny.* Oil on canvas, 81 x 92 cm, 1900. Musée d'Orsay, Paris
1a*r Weeping Willow.* Oil on canvas, 100 x 120 cm, 1918–9. Musée Marmottan, Paris
1b*l Water Lily Pool, Green Harmony.* Oil on canvas, 89 x 93 cm, 1899. Musée d'Orsay, Paris
1b*r Blue Water Lilies.* Oil on canvas, 200 x 200 cm, undated. *Ibid.*
2 *Path in the garden at Giverny.* Autochrome by Etienne Clémentel, c. 1917. *Ibid.*
3 *The Garden at Giverny.* Oil on canvas, 81 x 92 cm, 1900. *Ibid.*
4 *Monet beside the water lily pool.* Autochrome by Etienne Clémentel, c. 1917. *Ibid.*
5 *Water Lily Pool, Green Harmony* (detail). Oil on canvas, 89 x 93 cm, 1899. *Ibid.*
6 *Water lily pool at Giverny.* Autochrome, c. 1917

7 *Weeping Willow* (detail). Oil on canvas, 100 x 120 cm, 1918–9. Musée Marmottan, Paris
8 *Water lily pool at Giverny* (detail). Autochrome, 1917
9 *Blue Water Lilies* (detail). Oil on canvas, 200 x 200 cm, undated. Musée d'Orsay, Paris
11 *Poppies.* Oil on canvas, 50 x 65 cm, 1873. *Ibid.*
12 *The Beach at Sainte-Adresse* (detail). Oil on canvas, 75.8 x 102.5 cm, 1867. Art Institute of Chicago, Mr. and Mrs. Lewis Larned Coburn Memorial Collection
13 *Monet* c. 1860. Photograph by Carjat. J.-M. Toulgouat Collection
14a *Dandy with Monocle.* Tinted drawing, 24 x 16 cm, 1857. Musée Marmottan, Paris
14b *Caricatures.* Black pencil and gouache, c. 1858. *Ibid.*
15*l* Photograph of the port of Le Havre, France, c. 1860
15*r Man in a Boater.* Tinted drawing, 24 x 16 cm, 1857. Musée Marmottan, Paris
16a *The François I Tower and Semaphore at the Port Entrance, Le Havre.* Drawing, c. 1856. Private collection
16b*l Eugène Boudin Working at Le Havre.* Pencil on gray paper, c. 1857. Musée Eugène Boudin, Honfleur, France
17a *Landscape at Rouelles.* Oil on canvas, 46 x 65 cm, 1858. Private collection
17b *Eugène Boudin. Boats at Low Tide.* Drawing. Private collection

18a *The Pavé de Chailly.* Oil on canvas, 43.5 x 55 cm, c. 1865. Musée d'Orsay, Paris
18b Catalogue cover for the Salon of 1865
19 *Edouard Manet. Le Déjeuner sur l'Herbe.* Oil on canvas, 208.3 x 264.2 cm, 1863. Musée d'Orsay, Paris
20*r The Picnic,* left panel. Oil on canvas, 41.8 x 150 cm, 1865–6. *Ibid.*
20–1 Preparatory pencil sketch for *The Picnic,* 1865. Musée Marmottan, Paris
21a *The Picnic,* oil sketch. Oil on canvas, 130 x 181 cm, 1865–6. Pushkin Museum, Moscow
21b *The Picnic,* central panel. Oil on canvas, 248 x 217 cm, 1865–6. Musée d'Orsay, Paris
22 *Women in the Garden.* Oil on canvas, 256 x 208 cm, 1866–7. *Ibid.*
22–3 *Woman in a Green Dress* (and detail). Oil on canvas, 231 x 157 cm, 1866. Kunsthalle, Bremen, Germany
24 *The Green Wave.* Oil on canvas, 48.6 x 64.8 cm, 1865. Metropolitan Museum of Art, New York, bequest of Mrs. H. O. Havemeyer, 1929, the H. O. Havemeyer Collection
25a *Rough Sea at Etretat.* Oil on canvas, 66 x 131 cm, 1868–9. Musée d'Orsay, Paris
25b *Cliffs and the Sea.* Pencil, 20 x 31 cm, c. 1865. Art Institute of Chicago, Clarence Buckingham Collection
26–7 *The Terrace at Sainte-Adresse* (and details). Oil on canvas,

98.1 x 129.9 cm, 1867. Metropolitan Museum of Art, New York, purchased with special contributions and purchase funds given or bequeathed by friends of the Museum
28a *The Magpie.* Oil on canvas, 89 x 130 cm, 1869. Musée d'Orsay, Paris
28b *The Magpie* (detail)
29b*l Cart, Road under Snow, Honfleur.* Oil on canvas, 65 x 92.5 cm, c. 1867. *Ibid.*
29a*r The Magpie* (detail). *Ibid.*
30a *La Grenouillère.* Oil on canvas, 74.6 x 99.7 cm, 1869. Metropolitan Museum of Art, New York, bequest of Mrs. H. O. Havemeyer, 1929, the H. O. Havemeyer Collection
30b *Auguste Renoir. La Grenouillère.* Oil on canvas, 66 x 86 cm, 1869. Statens Konstmuseet, Stockholm
30–1 *La Grenouillère,* Chatou, France. Photograph, late 19th century
32a *Train in the Countryside.* Oil on canvas, 50 x 65 cm, c. 1870. Musée d'Orsay, Paris
32–3 *Train in the Countryside* (detail)
33a *Green Park.* Oil on canvas, 34 x 72 cm, 1871. Philadelphia Museum of Art, W. P. Wilstach Collection
34 *Poppies* (detail). Oil on canvas, 50 x 65 cm, 1873. Musée d'Orsay, Paris
35 *Monet,* about twenty-eight years old. Photograph. Monet Archives, Musée Marmottan, Paris
36a*l Lilacs in Dull Weather,* or *Resting Under the Lilacs.* Oil on canvas, 50 x 65.7 cm, 1872.

Musée d'Orsay, Paris
36ar *Lilacs in Sunshine.*
Oil on canvas, 50 x 65
cm, c. 1872–3. Pushkin
Museum, Moscow
36b *Lilacs in Dull
Weather* (detail). *Ibid.*
37 *Girl Reading.* Oil on
canvas, 50 x 65 cm,
c. 1872–4. Walters Art
Gallery, Baltimore
38a Detail of catalogue
cover of the First
Impressionist Exhibition,
1874
38b The First
Impressionist Exhibition
in 1874, cartoon by
Cham. BN
38–9 Title of an article
in *La Presse*, 1874
39 *Impression, Sunrise.*
Oil on canvas, 48 x 63
cm, 1872–3. Formerly
Musée Marmottan, Paris
40–1 *Luncheon.* Oil on
canvas, 160 x 201 cm,
c. 1873. Musée d'Orsay,
Paris
42a Edouard Manet. *The
Monet Family in the
Garden.* Oil on canvas,
61 x 99.7 cm, 1874.
Metropolitan Museum of
Art, New York, bequest of
Joan Whitney Payson,
1975
42bl Auguste Renoir.
*Mme. Monet and Her Son
in Their Garden.* Oil on
canvas, 51 x 68 cm, 1874.
National Gallery of Art,
Washington, D.C.
42br Auguste Renoir.
*Portrait of Mme. Claude
Monet.* Oil on canvas, 61
x 50 cm, 1872. Musée
Marmottan, Paris
43a Edouard Manet.
Head of a Man (Monet).
China ink wash, 1874.
Ibid.
43b Auguste Renoir.
Claude Monet Reading.
Oil on canvas, 61 x
50 cm, 1872. *Ibid.*
44a Edouard Manet.
*Monet Painting in His
Studio-Boat at Argenteuil.*

Oil on canvas, 81.3 x
99.7 cm, 1874. Neue
Pinakothek, Munich
44bl *The Studio-Boat.*
Oil on canvas, 50 x
64 cm, c. 1874. Kröller-
Müller Museum, Otterlo,
the Netherlands
44br *Regattas at
Argenteuil* (detail). Oil on
canvas, 48 x 75 cm, 1872.
Musée d'Orsay, Paris
44–5 *Idem* (with details)
46–7 *The Artist's House at
Argenteuil.* Oil on canvas,
60.2 x 73.3 cm, 1873. Art
Institute of Chicago,
Mr. and Mrs. Martin A.
Ryerson Collection
47ar Auguste Renoir.
*Monet Painting in His
Garden at Argenteuil*
(detail). Oil on canvas,
50.2 x 106.7 cm,
c. 1875. Wadsworth
Atheneum, Hartford,
Connecticut, bequest of
Anne Parrish Titzell
47cr *The Artist's House at
Argenteuil* (detail)
47br *Idem*
48 *The Railway Bridge,
Argenteuil* (with details).
Oil on canvas, 54 x 71
cm, c. 1873. Musée
d'Orsay, Paris
49 *The Railway Bridge,
Argenteuil* (with details).
Oil on canvas, 54.5 x 73.5
cm, 1874. Philadelphia
Museum of Art, The John
G. Johnson Collection
50a Alice Hoschedé with
her son Jean-Pierre.
Photograph, 1878
50–1 *Turkeys* (and detail).
Oil on canvas, 174.5 x
172.5 cm, 1876–7. Musée
d'Orsay, Paris
52 *Rue Montorgueil, Fête
of 30 June 1878* (detail).
Oil on canvas, 80 x 50
cm, 1878. *Ibid.*
53 Monet. Photograph,
c. 1875. Galerie
Bernheim-Jeune, Paris
54 The Pont-Neuf.
Photograph, 19th century
55a *Saint-Germain*

l'Auxerrois. Oil on canvas,
79 x 98 cm, 1867.
National Gallery,
Staatliche Museen
Preussischer
Kulturbesitz, Berlin
55b Auguste Renoir.
Photograph, c. 1875.
Musée d'Orsay, Paris
56 *Boulevard des
Capucines* (with detail).
Oil on canvas, 79.4 x
60.6 cm, 1873. Nelson-
Atkins Museum of Art,
Kansas City (acquired
through Kenneth A. and
Helen F. Spencer Foun-
dation Acquisition Fund)
57a *Boulevard des
Capucines.* Oil on canvas,
61 x 80 cm, 1873.
Pushkin Museum, Moscow
57b Frédéric Bazille. *Self-
Portrait in Chalk.* Musée
du Louvre, Paris
58 *La Japonaise.* Oil on
canvas, 231.6 x 142.3 cm,
1875–6. Museum of Fine
Arts, Boston, 1951
Purchase Fund
59 *Parc Monceau.* Oil on
canvas, 72.7 x 54.3 cm,
1878. Metropolitan
Museum of Art, New
York, Mr. and Mrs. Henry
Ittleson, Jr., Fund, 1959
60 *The Gare Saint-
Lazare, Exterior.* Oil on
canvas, 64 x 81 cm, 1877.
Private collection, France
61al *The Gare Saint-
Lazare, the Arrival of a
Train.* Oil on canvas, 83.1
x 101.5 cm, 1877. Fogg
Art Museum, Harvard
University Art Museums,
Cambridge, Massachusetts,
Collection of Maurice
Wertheim
61ar *The Pont de l'Europe,
Gare Saint-Lazare.* Oil on
canvas, 64 x 81 cm, 1877.
Musée Marmottan, Paris
61b Sketch for *The Gare
Saint-Lazare, the Arrival of
a Train.* Pencil on paper.
Ibid.
62–3 *The Gare Saint-
Lazare.* Oil on canvas,

75.5 x 104 cm, 1877.
Musée d'Orsay, Paris
64l Edouard Manet.
Photograph by Nadar,
c. 1864
64–5 *Rue Montorgueil,
Fête of 30 June 1878.* Oil
on canvas, 80 x 50 cm,
1878. Musée d'Orsay,
Paris
65a Third Impressionist
Exhibition, caricature by
Cham in *Le Charivari*,
April 1877. BN
66 *The Seine at Vétheuil.*
Oil on canvas, 81 x 60
cm, 1879. Musée des
Beaux-Arts, Rouen
67 Monet. Photograph by
Benque and Co., c. 1879.
BN
68 *The Church at Vétheuil,
Snow.* Oil on canvas, 52 x
71 cm, 1878–9. Musée
d'Orsay, Paris
69a *The Seine at
Vétheuil, Effect of Sunshine
After Rain.* Oil on canvas,
60 x 81 cm, 1879. *Ibid.*
69b View of the village
of Vétheuil. Photograph,
late 19th century
70al *Chrysanthemums.*
Oil on canvas, 54 x
65 cm, 1878. Musée
d'Orsay, Paris
70–1 *Camille Monet on
Her Deathbed.* Oil on
canvas, 90 x 68 cm, 1879.
Ibid.
71 Camille Monet. Photograph by A. Greiner, 1871
72 *Ice Floes Near
Vétheuil.* Oil on canvas,
65 x 93 cm, 1880.
Louvre, Collection H. and
V. Lyon, Paris
73 *Ice Floes on the Seine.*
Oil on canvas, 60 x
100 cm, 1880. Musée
d'Orsay, Paris
74a *Lavacourt.* Oil on
canvas, 100 x 150 cm,
1880. Dallas Museum of
Art, Texas
74b Emile Zola, studio
photograph, Benque
and Co.
75l Edouard Manet.

Théodore Duret (detail). Oil on canvas, 43.2 x 34.9 cm, 1868. Musée du Petit Palais, Paris

75r Cover of Monet exhibition catalogue, 1880, published by Georges Charpentier

76 *The Artist's Garden at Vétheuil.* Oil on canvas, 150 x 120 cm, 1881. National Gallery of Art, Washington, D.C., Collection Ailsa Mellon Bruce

77 *Spring.* Oil on canvas, 60 x 79 cm, 1880. Musée des Beaux-Arts, Lyon, France

78a *Rough Sea at Etretat.* Oil on canvas, 81 x 100 cm, 1883. *Ibid.*

78b Signboard of the Durand-Ruel Gallery, rue de la Paix. Durand-Ruel Archives, Paris

79a List of works bought by Durand-Ruel, manuscript in Monet's handwriting, 13 January 1884. *Ibid.*

79b Paul Durand-Ruel in his gallery. Photograph, c. 1910. *Ibid.*

80 *The Cliffs Near Dieppe.* Oil on canvas, 66 x 82 cm, 1882. Kunsthaus, Zurich, Association of Friends of Art, Zurich

80–1b Letter from Monet to Paul Durand-Ruel, manuscript dated 20 December 1881. Durand-Ruel Archives, Paris

81 *Cliff Walk at Pourville.* Oil on canvas, 66.5 x 82.3 cm, 1882. Art Institute of Chicago, Mr. and Mrs. Lewis Larned Coburn Memorial Collection

82 *Boat at Giverny* (detail). Oil on canvas, 98 x 131 cm, c. 1887. Musée d'Orsay, Paris

83 Monet. Photograph by painter Theodore

Robinson, c. 1887. Durand-Ruel Archives, Paris

84al Vegetation at Bordighera. Detail of photograph, 19th century

84ar *Villas at Bordighera* (detail). Oil on canvas, 73 x 92 cm, 1884. Santa Barbara Museum of Art, bequest of Katherine Dexter McCormick in memory of her husband, Stanley McCormick

84b *Etretat.* Pencil drawing, Musée Marmottan, Paris

85a *Villas at Bordighera*

85bl Palm trees at Bordighera. Detail of a photograph

85br *Villas at Bordighera* (detail)

86 *Tulip Fields at Sassenheim Neur Haarlem* (details and whole). Oil on canvas, 59.7 x 73.2 cm, 1886. Sterling and Francine Clark Art Institute, Williamstown, Massachusetts

86–7c Page from Monet's address book, autograph manuscript, undated. Musée Marmottan, Paris

88a *The "Pyramides" of Port-Coton.* Oil on canvas, 65 x 81 cm, 1886. Private collection

88b *The "Pyramides" of Port-Coton, Belle-Ile,* France. Detail of a photograph, late 19th century

88–9 *Belle-Ile.* Oil on canvas, 65 x 85.5 cm, 1886. Musée Rodin, Paris

90l *Antibes Seen from the Cap.* Oil on canvas, 65 x 81 cm, 1888. Private collection

90r *Antibes Seen from the Cap* (details). *Ibid.*

91a *Antibes Seen from La Salis.* Detail of a photograph, late 19th century

91b *Antibes Seen from La Salis.* Oil on canvas, 65 x

92 cm, 1888. Private collection, New York

92 *Creuse Valley at Dusk.* Oil on canvas, 65 x 81 cm, 1889. Musée Saint-Denis, Rheims, France

93a *Creuse Valley, Evening Effect.* Oil on canvas, 65 x 81 cm, 1889. Musée Marmottan, Paris

93b *Creuse Valley, Sunset.* Oil on canvas, 74 x 70.5 cm, 1889. Unterlinden Museum, Colmar, France

94a Catalogue cover for the Monet-Rodin Exhibition, 1889. Georges Petit Gallery, Paris

94bl Auguste Rodin in his studio. Photograph, c. 1887

94–5 Auguste Rodin. *The Burghers of Calais.* Photograph by Théodore Duret, 1896–8. Musée Rodin, Paris

95a Edouard Manet. *Olympia.* Oil on canvas, 130.5 x 190 cm, 1863. Musée d'Orsay, Paris

96a *Study of a Boat.* Pencil on paper, c. 1887. Musée Marmottan, Paris

96b *The Boat.* Oil on canvas, 146 x 133 cm, 1887. *Ibid.*

97 *Boat at Giverny,* or *In the "Norvégienne."* Oil on canvas, 98 x 131 cm, 1887. Musée d'Orsay, Paris

98 *Woman with Parasol Facing Right.* Oil on canvas, 131 x 88 cm, 1886. *Ibid.*

99al *Woman with Parasol Facing Left.* Oil on canvas, 131 x 88 cm, 1886. *Ibid.*

99ar *The Promenade.* Oil on canvas, 100 x 81 cm, 1875. National Gallery of Art, Washington, D.C., gift of Mr. and Mrs. Paul Mellon

99b *Lady with Parasol.* Pencil on paper, c. 1886

100 *Effect of Wind,* Poplars series. Oil on canvas, 100 x 74 cm,

1891. Private collection, France

101 Monet. Photograph by Sardnal, 1897. *Ibid.*

102 *Poppy Fields, Giverny.* Oil on canvas, 61.2 x 93.1 cm, 1890–1. Art Institute of Chicago, Mr. and Mrs. W. W. Kimball Collection, 1922

103l *Idem* (detail)

103r Study of haystacks. Pencil on paper, c. 1890. Musée Marmottan, Paris

104a *Haystacks Late Summer, Morning Effect.* Oil on canvas, 60.5 x 100.5 cm, 1890–1. Musée d'Orsay, Paris

104b *Haystacks, Effect of Snow, Morning.* Oil on canvas, 64.5 x 92.3 cm, 1890–1. Gift of Misses Aimée and Rosamond Lamb in memory of Mr. and Mrs. Horatio A. Lamb. Museum of Fine Arts, Boston

105a *Haystacks, Late Summer, Morning Effect* (details). *Ibid.*

105b *Haystacks, Effect of Snow, Morning* (details)

106–7 *Haystacks, Effect of Snow, Dull Weather.* Oil on canvas, 66 x 93 cm, 1890–1. Art Institute of Chicago, Mr. and Mrs. Martin A. Ryerson Collection

108a *Haystacks, Late Summer, Evening Effect.* Oil on canvas, 60 x 100 cm, 1890–1. Art Institute of Chicago, Arthur M. Wood in memory of Pauline Palmer Wood

108b *Haystack, Melting Snow, Sunset.* Oil on canvas, 64.9 x 92.3 cm, 1890–1. Art Institute of Chicago, gift of Mr. and Mrs. Daniel C. Searle, 1983

109a *Haystacks, Late Summer, Evening Effect* (details). *Ibid.*

109b *Haystack, Melting Snow, Sunset* (details)

110–1 Poplars, Three Pink Trees, Autumn (and details). Oil on canvas, 36 x 29 cm, 1891. Philadelphia Museum of Art: Given by Chester Dale

112l Rouen Cathedral, the Portal and the Tour Saint-Romain: Morning Effect, Harmony in White. Oil on canvas, 106 x 75 cm, 1892–4. Musée d'Orsay, Paris

112r Rouen Cathedral: Sun Effect, End of the Day. Oil on canvas, 100 x 65 cm, 1892. Musée Marmottan, Paris

113l Rouen Cathedral: Morning Sunlight, Harmony in Blue. Oil on canvas, 91 x 63 cm, 1894. Musée d'Orsay, Paris

113r Rouen Cathedral: Symphony in Gray and Pink. Oil on canvas, 100 x 65 cm, 1894. National Museum of Wales, Cardiff

114–5 From the magazine *Le Gaulois,* 16 June 1898

115ar The Fisherman's House, Varengeville. Oil on wood, 60 x 78 cm, 1882. Boymans-van Beuningen Museum, Rotterdam, the Netherlands

115b Cliff at Varengeville. Oil on canvas, 65 x 92 cm, 1897. Musée des Beaux-Arts, Le Havre, France

116 The Houses of Parliament: Sun Shining Through a Gap in the Fog. Oil on canvas, 81 x 92 cm, 1904. Musée d'Orsay, Paris

116–7 List of views of the Thames, London, 1900–4, written by Monet. Durand-Ruel Archives, Paris

117 The Houses of Parliament: Stormy Sky. Oil on canvas, 81 x 92 cm, 1904. Musée des Beaux Arts, Lille, France

118a Sketch of the Palazzo Dario, Venice. Pencil on paper, undated.

Musée Marmottan, Paris

118b Cover of the *Venice* album by Monet, Galerie Bernheim-Jeune, Paris, 1912

118–9 The Doges' Palace Seen from San Giorgio Maggiore. Oil on canvas, 65.4 x 92.7 cm, 1908. Metropolitan Museum of Art, New York, gift of Mr. and Mrs. Charles S. McVeigh, 1959

120 Water Lilies—Water Landscape. Oil on canvas, 100.5 x 73.4 cm, 1907. Bridgestone Museum of Art, Ishibashi Foundation, Tokyo

121 Monet at Giverny. Photograph by Sacha Guitry, c. 1920

122l The Water Lily Pool: Harmony in Pink. Oil on canvas, 89.5 x 100 cm, 1900. Musée d'Orsay, Paris

122r The water lily pool at Giverny. Detail of an autochrome by Etienne Clémentel, c. 1917. *Ibid.*

123a The Japanese Bridge. Oil on canvas, 89.5 x 116.5 cm, c. 1923. Minneapolis Institute of Art, Minnesota

123b Water Lilies. Oil on canvas, 80 cm diameter, 1907. Musée d'Art Moderne de Saint-Etienne, France

124l Extract from catalogue of the exhibition "Les Nymphéas, a Series of Water Landscapes," 1909, Durand-Ruel Gallery. Durand-Ruel Archives, Paris

124r Portrait of the Artist. Oil on canvas, 70 x 55 cm, 1917. Musée d'Orsay, Paris

125l Sketch of a flower (marked "pale mauve"), from Monet's sketchbook. Musée Marmottan, Paris

125r List of flower names, manuscript from Monet's sketchbook. *Ibid.*

126–7 Monet in his last

studio at Giverny. Photograph by Henri Manuel, c. 1920. Durand-Ruel Archives, Paris

128 and gatefolds Panels of Water Lilies in the Musée de l'Orangerie, Paris. Recto: *Morning, No. 1* (left and central sections), c. 1916–26, each panel 200 x 425 cm, Room 2, north wall; Verso: *The Clouds* (right-hand section), c. 1916–26, Room 1, north wall

129 Monet's signature

130 Extract from Monet's address book, undated manuscript. Musée Marmottan, Paris

132 Frédéric Bazille. Photograph, undated

133 Edouard Manet. Photograph by Carjat, c. 1880

134 Berthe Morisot in her studio. Photograph, undated. *Ibid.*

135 Paul Cézanne with his painting *The Bathers* (detail). Photograph by Emile Bernard, 1904. *Ibid.*

136 Camille Pissarro. Self-portrait. Drawing. BN

138 Monet with two friends in his garden at Giverny. Photograph, undated. Musée Marmottan, Paris

139 Frédéric Bazille. *Portrait of Auguste Renoir.* Oil on canvas, 24.5 x 20 cm, 1867. Musée d'Orsay, Paris

141 Wassily Kandinsky in Munich. Photograph, c. 1913. Musée National d'Art Moderne, Paris

144 Emile Zola. Photograph, undated

146 Guy de Maupassant. Photograph by Nadar, c. 1890. *Ibid.*

148 Octave Mirbeau. Photograph by Studio Reutlinger, c. 1900. *Ibid.*

149 Georges Clemenceau and Monet at Giverny (acted by Jean Périer and Sacha Guitry), scene from Sacha Guitry's play *Histoire de France,* cover of *Vu,* 16 October 1929

152 Monet retouching a painting in his studio. Photograph, 1920. Musée d'Orsay, Paris

154 Monet with Anna Bergman and Jacques Hoschedé in his second studio. Photograph, c. 1900. Collection Philippe Piguet

156l Georges Clemenceau, Monet, and Lily Butler on the Japanese bridge in the garden at Giverny. Photograph, June 1921. Collection J.-M. Toulgouat

156–7 Family reunion at Giverny. Photograph, end of the 19th century. *Ibid.*

158 The garden at Giverny. Photograph, end of the 19th century

159 Menu for Germaine Hoschedé's wedding luncheon, 12 November 1902, manuscript by Monet. Collection J.-M. Toulgouat

160 Monet and Gustave Geffroy at Giverny. Photograph by Sacha Guitry, c. 1920

161 The water lily pond. Photograph, c. 1895

162 Monet painting panels of Water Lilies at Giverny. Photograph, 1920

164al Georges Clemenceau. Photograph by Henri Manuel, c. 1900

164–5 Plan of the Orangerie, May 1927. Archives Nationales, Paris

165 The Orangerie, with Monet's Water Lilies. Photograph, c. 1930

166–7 Visitors to the Water Lilies at the Orangerie, Paris. Photograph, 1930

Index

*Page numbers in italics
refer to captions and/or
illustrations.*

A

Alexandre, Arsène 143
*Antibes Seen from La Salis
91*
*Antibes Seen from the Cap
90*
Arnyvelde, André 154
*The Artist's Garden at
Vétheuil 76*
*The Artist's House at
Argenteuil 46–7*
*Avenue in the Park,
Montgeron* see *The Hunt*

B

Bazille, Frédéric 18, 19,
20, 21, 22, 23, 24, 25,
27, 28, *28,* 29, *29,* 31,
32, 38, 48, 54, 55, *57,*
132, 139, 155
*The Beach at Sainte-
Adresse 12*
Belle-Ile 88–9
Bellio, Georges de 48, 50,
58, 68, 70, *72,* 77, *87*
Benois, Alexandre 165
Bernard, Emile 140
Bernheim-Jeune, G. *124,*
125, 150, 154, 155,
157, 158
Bernheim-Jeune Gallery
116, 118
Bernheim-Jeune, J. *124,*
125, 150, 154
The Boat 96
Boat at Giverny 82, 97
Boudin, Eugène 15, 16,
16, 17, 23, 28, 35, 36,
39, 54, 55, 86, 131
Boulevard des Capucines
39, 56, *57,* 65
Boussod-Valadon Gallery
90, 102, 110, 113
Butor, Michel 166

C

Caillebotte, Gustave 48,
50, 51, 57, 58, 64, 68,

87, 89, 125, 138, 155,
159
*Camille Monet on Her
Deathbed 70–1*
Camoin, Charles 136
*Cart, Road Under Snow,
Honfleur 28–9*
Cassatt, Mary 88
Cézanne, Paul 39, 74, 84,
124, 135–6
Charteris, Evan 153
Chrysanthemums 70
*The Church at Vétheuil,
Snow 68*
Cladel, Judith 143
Claudel, Paul 163
Clemenceau, Georges *71,*
89, 97, *102, 103,* 114,
114, 123, 124, *124,*
125, 126, 127, *127,*
150, 151, 155, *156,*
158, 159, *164*
Cliff at Varengeville 115
Cliffs and the Sea 24–5
The Cliffs Near Dieppe 80
*The Cliff Walk at Pourville
81*
*Corner of a Garden at
Montgeron 50*
Courbet, Gustave 20, *21,*
28, 86, 132
Creuse Valley at Dusk 92
*Creuse Valley, Evening
Effect 93*
Creuse Valley, Sunset 93

D

Daubigny, Charles-
François 16, 25, 31,
32, 130, 132
Degas, Edgar 38, 39,
126, 140
Déjeuner sur l'Herbe
(Manet) 18, *19*
Denis, Maurice 141
Dewhurst, Wynford 161
*Doges' Palace Seen from San
Giorgio Maggiore 118*
d'Ors, Eugenio 165
Durand-Ruel, Joseph
123, 140; Paul 32–3,
37, 43, 48, 75, 77, 78,
79, 79–80, 81, *81,* 84,
85, 87, 92, 102, 103,

110, 111, 113, 114,
114, 117, *117, 122,*
123, 124, 125, 126,
130, 133, 142, 153, 154
Duret, Théodore 38, 65,
68, 73, 74, *74, 75,* 77,
83, *84,* 90, *98,* 143,
145–6, 152

E

Effect of Wind (Poplars
series) *100*

F

Fallières, Armand 134
Faure, Jean-Baptiste 43,
48, 77, *87*
Fénéon, Félix 140
*The Fisherman's House,
Varengeville 115*

G

The Garden in Flower 36
The Gare Saint-Lazare
series 50, *60–1, 62–3,*
64
Gasquet, Joachim 136
Gautier, Armand 15, 16,
23, 54, 56
Geffroy, Gustave *17,*
53, *53,* 89, *89,* 91,
92, *92,* 94, 101, 103,
109, 118, *119,* 124,
126, 127, 136, 139,
144, 149, 150, 151,
152, 154, 155, 157,
158, 159, *160*
Girl Reading 37
Gleyre, Charles 18
Green Park 33
The Green Wave 24
La Grenouillère 30, 31, *31*
Guitry, Sacha *121,* 124,
149, 157, 158

H

Hamerton, Philip 151
*Haystack, Melting Snow,
Sunset 108–9*
*Haystacks, Effect of Snow,
Dull Weather 106–7*
Haystacks, Effect of Snow,

Morning 104–5
*Haystacks, Late Summer,
Evening Effect 108–9*
*Haystacks, Late Summer,
Morning Effect 104–5*
Haystacks series 102,
103, *103, 105, 109,*
110, *111, 113*
Hoschedé, Alice *see*
Monet, Alice
Hoschedé, Blanche *82,
9?,* 114, 116, *127;*
Ernest 43, 49–50, 58,
68, 75, 112; Germaine
97, 159; Jean Pierre
50, *50,* 160; Suzanne
82, 97, 98, 99, 112, 126
*The Houses of Parliament:
Stormy Sky 117*
*The Houses of Parliament:
Sun Shining Through a
Gap in the Fog 116*
The Hunt 50

I

Ice Floes on the Seine 73
Ice Floes paintings 67,
72, 92
Impression, Sunrise
38, *38,* 39, 43, *117*

J

The Japanese Bridge 123
La Japonaise 58, 58
*Jeanne-Marguerite Lecadre
in the Garden 36*
Jongkind, Johan Barthold
17, 131
Joyant, Maurice 110, 113,
160

K

Kandinsky, Wassily 141–2

L

*Landscape at Rouelles 16,
17*
Lavacourt 73, 74
Lecadre, Jeanne-
Marguerite *26–7;*
Marie-Jeanne 14, 15,
18, *26–7,* 31

Leroy, Louis *38*, 39, *56*, 57, *57*
Levens, H. M. 140
Lilacs in Dull Weather 36
Lilacs in Sunshine 36
Luncheon 40–1
Lysès, Charlotte 157, 158

M

The Magpie *28*, 30
Maillol, Aristide 143
Mallarmé, Stéphane 48, 91, *109*, 122, 124, 126, 133, 147, 158, 159
Manet, Edouard 18, *19*, 37, 38, 42, *42*, 43, *43*, *44*, 58, 64, *64*, 65, 70, *75*, 84, *95*, 96, 132–4
Manet, Julie 139
Mantz, Paul 13, 19
Martin, F. ("Père") 131
Masson, André 166–7
Mauclair, Camille 163–4
Maupassant, Guy de 85, 90, 91, 146, *146*
May, Ernest 48, 58, 64
Mirbeau, Octave 90, 94, 98, 99, *99*, 118, 124, 126, 147–8, 153
Monet, Adolphe 14, 16
Monet, Alice (Hoschedé) 49, 50, *50*, 68, 70, 75, 80, *81*, 84, 88, 89, 92, 97, 111, 112, 116, 117, 118, 119, 126, 135, 148, 153, 156, 157
Monet, Camille (Doncieux) 22, *22–3*, 24, 25, 28, 31, 32, *35*, 36, 39, *42*, 43, 55, 64, 67, 70–1, *71*, 72, 75, *99*
Monet, Jean 25, 28, *35*, 36, *40–1*, 43, 64, 97, 127
Monet, Louise-Justine 14
Monet, Michel 64–5, 70, 97
The Monet Family in the Garden (Manet) 42
Monet Painting in His Garden at Argenteuil (Renoir) *47*

Monet Painting in His Studio-Boat (Manet) *44*
Moreau-Nélaton, Etienne 130
Morisot, Berthe 39, 87, 88, 91, 92, 97, 98, 124, 126, 134–5
Morning on the Seine series 115
Mount Kolsaas series 114
The Mouth of the Seine at Honfleur 13

N

Nadar (Félix Tournachon) 39, *56*, 57, 143
Nadar, Paul 143
Nymphéas *see* Water Lilies series

O

Ochard, Jean-François 14, 28
Ozenfant, Amédée 166

P

Palazzo Dario (Venice) 118
Parc Monceau 58, *59*
The Pavé de Chailly 18
Petit, Georges 77, 86, 87, *87*, 93, 94, 115
Pissarro, Camille 16, 33, 36, 38, 39, 57, 71, 91, 103, *111*, 115, 124, 126, 136–7
Pissarro, Lucien 103, 136–7
The Pointe de la Hève at Low Tide 13
The Pont-Neuf 56
The Pool at Montgeron 50
Poplars, Three Pink Trees, Autumn 110–1
Poplars series *100*, 110, *110–1*, 117
Poppies 34, 39
Poppy Fields series 102, *102*, *111*

The Promenade 99
Proust, Marcel 60, *73*, 118, 121, 147
The "Pyramides" of Port-Coton, Belle-Ile 88

R

The Railway Bridge, Argenteuil 48
Regattas at Argenteuil 44–5
Renoir, Auguste 18, 24, *30*, 31, *31*, 38, 39, 43, *43*, *47*, 48, 54, *55*, 56, 58, 73, 74, 84, 124, 126, 139
Rodin, Auguste *89*, 90, 94–5, *94–5*, 124, 142–3, 148
Rolland, Romain 148–9
Rouen Cathedral, Effect of Sunshine, End of the Day 112
Rouen Cathedral, Harmony in Brown 125
Rouen Cathedral, Morning Sunlight, Harmony in Blue 113
Rouen Cathedral, the Portal and the Tour Saint-Romain: Morning Effect, Harmony in White 112
Rouen Cathedral series 112–4, *112*, *113*
Rouen Cathedral Symphony in Grey and Pink 113
Rough Sea at Etretat (1868–9) 25
Rough Sea at Etretat (1883) 79
Rue Montorgueil *52*, 65, 64–5
Rue Saint-Denis 65

S

Saint-Germain l'Auxerrois 55
The Seine at Vétheuil 66; *Effect of Sunshine After Rain* 69
Signac, Paul 140–1

Sisley, Alfred 18, 38, 39, 48, 74, 124, 126, 139
The Studio Boat 44–5

T

The Terrace at Sainte-Adresse 24, *26–7*, 45
Train in the Countryside 32
Troyon, Constant 16, 130
Tuileries 58
Tulip Fields at Sassenheim Near Haarlem 86–7,
Tulip Fields paintings 86, 92
Turkeys 50, *51*

V

Van der Kemp, Gérald 161
Van Gogh, Theo *87*, 90, 110, 140
Van Gogh, Vincent 90, 140
Venice 117–8
Views of the Thames series 117, *117*
Views of Vétheuil series 122
Villas at Bordighera 84–5

W

Water Lilies series 122–3, *122*, *123*, *128 recto and verso*, 154
The Water Lily Pool: Harmony in Pink 122
Woman in a Green Dress 22, *22–3*, 30
Women in the Garden 22, 23, 24, 125
Woman with Parasol Facing Left 99
Woman with Parasol Facing Right 98

Z

Zola, Emile *23*, 28, *32*, *36*, *37*, 48, 60, *63*, 65, 73, *74*, 144–5

Acknowledgments

The author is especially grateful to Marianne Delafond (Musée Marmottan), Caroline Durand-Ruel Godfroy (Archives Durand-Ruel), Françoise Heilbrun (Musée d'Orsay), Jacqueline Henry (Documentation), Michel Hoog (Musée de l'Orangerie), Philippe Piguet, Claire Joyes, and Jean-Marie Toulgouat (archive photographs), the Wildenstein Foundation, the Photographic Service of the Réunion des Musées Nationaux, and Gérard Patin for their help in the preparation of this volume. The publishers wish to thank the Bernheim-Jeune Gallery and the Durand-Ruel Gallery, Paris, and Claire Joyes, Jean-Marie Toulgouat, and Philippe Piguet for their kind assistance.

Photograph Credits

All rights reserved 16a, 17a, 17b, 18b, 38a, 38–9, 50a, 71, 75r, 88a, 94a, 94bl, 99b, 114–5. A.P.N., Paris 21a, 36ar, 57a. Archives Durand-Ruel, Paris 78b, 79a, 79b, 80–1b, 83, 101, 116–7, 124l, 126–7. Archives Nationales, Paris 164–5. Archives Tallandier, Paris 65a. Archiv für Kunst und Geschichte, Berlin 115ar. Artephot/Bridgeman 74a. Artephot/Held 44a, 44bl. Art Institute of Chicago 12, 25b, 46–7, 47bl, 47cr, 81, 102, 103l, 104a, 104b, 105a, 105b, 106–7. Bildarchiv Preussischer Kulturbesitz, Berlin 55a. Bridgeman Art Gallery, London 22–3, 23r, 37, 123a. Bridgestone Museum of Art, Ishibashi Foundation, Tokyo 120. Bulloz, Paris 92, 158, 161. Centre Georges Pompidou, Musée National d'Art Moderne, Kandinsky Foundation, Paris 139. Jean-Loup Charmet, Paris 35, 38–9, 67, 138, 149. Edimedia, Paris 90l, 90r, 136. Ellebé, Rouen 66. Fogg Art Museum, Harvard University Art Museums, Cambridge, Massachusetts 61al. Galerie Bernheim-Jeune, Paris 53, 118b. Giraudon/Lauros 117. Giraudon/Musée des Beaux-Arts du Havre 115b. Giraudon/Musée du Petit Palais, Paris 75l. L'Illustration/Sygma, Paris 6, 8. © Bruno Jarret by ADAGP and © Musée Rodin, Paris 88–9. Kunsthaus, Zurich, Association des Amis de l'Art Zurichois 80. Metropolitan Museum of Art, New York 24, 26–7, 30a, 42a, 59, 118–9. Musée d'Art Moderne de Saint-Etienne/Yves Bresson 123b. Musée des Beaux-Arts de Lyon 77, 78a. Musée Municipal de Honfleur 16bl. Musée Rodin, Paris 94–5. Musée d'Unterlinden/O. Zimmermann, Colmar 93b. Museum of Fine Arts, Boston 58, 108b, 109b. National Gallery of Art, Washington, D.C. 42bl, 76, 99ar. National Museum of Wales, Cardiff 113r. Nelson-Atkins Museum of Art, Kansas City 56. Philadelphia Museum of Art 33a, 49, 110–1. Philippe Piguet Collection 154. Private collection, France 60, 100. Private collection, New York 91b. Réunion des Musées Nationaux, Paris 1al, 1bl, 1br, 2, 3, 4, 5, 9, 11, 18a, 19, 20r, 21b, 22, 25a, 25b, 28a, 29, 32a, 32–3, 34, 36al, 36b, 40–1, 44–5, 52, 55b, 57b, 62–3, 64–5, 68, 69a, 70al, 70–1, 72, 73, 82, 95a, 97, 98, 99al, 108a, 109a, 112l, 113l, 116, 122l, 122r, 124r, 128 recto and verso, 139, 152, front cover, spine. Roger-Viollet 132. Roger-Viollet/Cap 69b. Roger-Viollet/Harlingue 160, 162, 165, 166–7. Roger-Viollet/ND 88b. Jean-Michel Routhier 1ar, 7, 14a, 14b, 15r, 20–1, 39, 42br, 43a, 43b, 61ar, 61b, 84b, 86–7c, 93a, 96a, 96b, 103r, 112r, 114–5, 118a, 125l, 125r, 130, back cover. Santa Barbara Museum of Art 84ar, 85a, 85br. Sipa Archives, Paris 30–1. Sirot/Angel Collection, Paris 15l, 54, 64l, 74b, 84al, 85bl, 91a, 121, 133, 134, 135, 144, 146, 148, 164al. Statens Konstmuseet, Stockholm 30b. Sterling and Francine Clark Art Institute, Williamstown, Massachusetts 86a, 86b. Studio Lourmel 77. Jean-Marie Toulgouat Collection 13, 156l, 156–7, 159. Wadsworth Atheneum, Hartford, Connecticut 47ar.

Text Credit

Grateful acknowledgment is made for use of material from Flint, Kate, ed., *Impressionists in England*, Routledge and Kegan Paul, London, 1984 (pp. 151, 160–1, and 163–4).

Sylvie Patin worked at the Jeu de Paume and the
Musée de l'Orangerie in Paris before being appointed
curator in the paintings department of the Musée d'Orsay.
She has helped organize several exhibitions, including
"Homage to Monet" (1980) and "Impressionism and the
French Landscape" (1985) at the Grand Palais and "Monet-
Rodin" (1989) at the Musée Rodin in Paris. Her recent
publications include *A la Campagne* (1986) and
Jardins d'Hier et d'Aujourd'hui (1991).

For Louis-Gabriel and Sophie

Translated from the French by Anthony Roberts

Project Manager: Sharon AvRutick
Typographic Designer: Elissa Ichiyasu
Cover Designer: Robert McKee
Editorial Assistant: Jennifer Stockman
Design Assistant: Penelope Hardy

Library of Congress Catalog Card Number: 92–82808

ISBN 0–8109–2883–3

Copyright © 1991 Gallimard/Réunion des Musées Nationaux

English translation copyright © 1993 Harry N. Abrams, Inc., New York,
and Thames and Hudson Ltd., London

Published in 1993 by Harry N. Abrams, Incorporated, New York

Printed and bound in Italy by Editoriale Lloyd, Trieste